Retrieval for the Sake of Renewal

Retrieval for the Sake of Renewal

Timothy George as a Historical Theologian

Christopher R. Hanna

Foreword by David S. Dockery
Afterword by Timothy George

WIPF & STOCK · Eugene, Oregon

RETRIEVAL FOR THE SAKE OF RENEWAL
Timothy George as a Historical Theologian

Copyright © 2022 Christopher R. Hanna. All rights reserved. Except for brief quotations in critical publications or reviews, no part of this book may be reproduced in any manner without prior written permission from the publisher. Write: Permissions, Wipf and Stock Publishers, 199 W. 8th Ave., Suite 3, Eugene, OR 97401.

Wipf & Stock
An Imprint of Wipf and Stock Publishers
199 W. 8th Ave., Suite 3
Eugene, OR 97401

www.wipfandstock.com

PAPERBACK ISBN: 978-1-6667-4845-1
HARDCOVER ISBN: 978-1-6667-4846-8
EBOOK ISBN: 978-1-6667-4847-5

11/15/22

Used with permission from Samford University's Beeson Divinity School, photographed by Kyle Thompson, originally published in the 2019 Beeson magazine

To Sara Adeli Hanna,
my beautiful and wonderful wife

What you have received as heritage,
take now as task, and thus you will make it your own.
—JOHANN WOLFGANG VON GOETHE

Contents

Foreword by David S. Dockery | ix
Acknowledgements | xiii

1 **Introduction** | 1
   The Influence of Timothy George | 1
   The Central Question | 5
   The Plan of This Book | 6

2 **Hell's Half Acre, Harvard, and Historical Theology** | 9
   Introduction | 9
   Chattanooga, Tennessee (1950–72) | 10
   Cambridge, Massachusetts (1972–78) | 17
   Louisville, Kentucky (1978–88) | 25
   Birmingham, Alabama (1988–present) | 30
   Conclusion | 34

3 **A Holy Calling, to Keep Truth Alive** | 36
   Introduction | 36
   Education and Career (1914–2000) | 37
   Major Contributions from George Huntston Williams | 40
   Reception and Transmission by Timothy George | 49
   Conclusion | 59

4 **The Quest to Free the Church from Amnesia** | 61
   Introduction | 61
   Education and Career (1936–2015) | 62
   Major Contributions from David Steinmetz | 66
   Reception and Transmission by Timothy George | 76
   Conclusion | 80

5 **Delighted by Doctrine** | 81
   Introduction | 81
   Education and Career (1923–2006) | 82
   Major Contributions from Jaroslav Pelikan | 87
   Reception and Transmission by Timothy George | 94
   Conclusion | 98

6 **Evangelical Ecumenism** | 100
   Introduction | 100
   The Hierarchy of Ecclesial Identity | 101
   The Essence of Timothy George's Historical Theology | 107
   The Implications of Timothy George's Historical Theology | 115
   Conclusion | 121
   Final Conclusion | 121

Afterword | 127
Appendix 1: Overview of Timothy George's Published Work | 133
Appendix 2: Selected Works by Williams, Steinmetz, and Pelikan | 141
Bibliography | 145

Foreword

THE STUDY OF HISTORICAL theology seeks to uncover, recover, and evaluate the work of scriptural interpretation as well as the formulation of Christian teaching throughout the history of the church. One of the most significant historical theologians of the past generation, Jaroslav Pelikan, has described historical theology as the study of what the church has believed, taught, and confessed as it has prayed, suffered, served, and obeyed, while celebrating and awaiting the coming of the kingdom of God.

Christopher Hanna has provided us with a wonderful introduction by viewing historical theology through the work of Timothy George, one of the premier historical theologians of this generation. Recognizing well and interacting capably with the stellar thinkers who have shaped and influenced the work of the founding dean of Beeson Divinity School, including Jaroslav Pelikan, Hanna, in the volume you hold in your hands, helps us to understand the importance of the role of historical theology as a servant to and for the church. In doing so, he leads us to see the goal of George's work as a historical theologian, beautifully captured in the title of this book, *Retrieval for the Sake of Renewal: Timothy George as a Historical Theologian.*

While best understood as an interpretive discipline and not an infallible one, historical theology serves faithful followers of Christ by helping us to see how the essential teachings of the Christian faith have been articulated and passed down from one generation to the next throughout the history of Christianity. In doing so, it helps believers distinguish between true and false teaching. It also serves as a ministerial and enabling guide in the interpretation of Scripture. Moreover, understanding this tradition and how it has developed through the years helps the church to have wisdom regarding the introduction of new teachings and approaches to ministry. In doing so, historical theologians seek to strengthen and equip believers so they will not be tossed to and fro by every wind of doctrine (Eph 4:13–16). Timothy George observed these patterns and offered wise warnings to those in attendance more than three decades ago in an address he gave at The Southern Baptist Theological Seminary called "Dogma Beyond Anathema: Historical Theology in Service to the Church." He noted that many assume recent modes of knowing truth are vastly superior to older ways, that the most recent proposals and trends must be the best. In response to this assumption, George contended that historical theology served as a bulwark against theological faddism. Such an approach has continued to inform George in his various roles for more than forty years.

A two-time Harvard graduate earning both the MDiv and ThD, Timothy George was privileged to study with the brilliant church historian George Huntston Williams. In addition to the informative roles of Williams and Pelikan, George was also influenced by Heiko Oberman and David Steinmetz. During this time, he was introduced to the shaping figures and movements throughout all of church history, while focusing his attention on Martin Luther, John Calvin, the Anabaptists, the English Reformation, and the Puritans. These historical writings became an anchor for George as his faith was stretched and challenged by other Harvard faculty members during his student days. Following his years at Harvard, George taught historical theology for a decade at Southern Seminary in Louisville, KY. In 1988, he was invited to become the founding dean at Beeson Divinity School on the campus of Samford University in Birmingham, AL, a role he carried out for more than three decades before recently being named Distinguished Professor of Divinity.

George's many years of studying the teachings of these shaping figures in the history of the church are evidenced in his numerous books, articles, and scholarly addresses. Examples of his publications include the highly praised *Theology of the Reformers* (1988/2013), a work that introduced readers to the thought of Luther, Calvin, Huldrych Zwingli, and Menno Simons. His edited work on *John Calvin and the Church* (1990) extended his reputation as a serious Reformation historian. Currently, George serves as the general editor of the multivolume *Reformation Commentary on Scripture*.

Foreword

His introductory volume to this important series, *Reading Scripture with the Reformers* (2011), engages the thought of Luther, Calvin, and other Reformers regarding their interpretation of Scripture, as does George's outstanding commentary on *Galatians* in the New American Commentary (1994, and revised for the Christian Standard Commentary in 2020).

The work of Timothy George as historical theologian extends beyond his expertise as Reformation scholar. He has also published important works on *John Robinson and the English Separatist Tradition* (1982), as well as James Petigru Boyce (1988), John Gill (1990), William Carey (1991), and D. L. Moody (2004), among others. His labors as a historical theologian have greatly informed his service as minister, preacher, administrator, and teacher. His theological contributions have primarily focused on the Trinitarian God, the doctrine of salvation, and the church.

An edited volume on *God the Holy Trinity* (2006) followed his excellent exposition of the Trinity a few years earlier in a response to the rise of Islam (*Is the Father of Jesus the God of Muhammed*). A more systematic expression appeared in his chapter on "The Nature of God: Being, Attributes, and Acts," which appeared in *A Theology for the Church* (2007/2014). He also authored a book on the doctrine of salvation, *Amazing Grace: God's Initiative—Our Response*. In addition, he has offered valuable insights along the way on Christian spirituality, evangelicalism, and Baptist life and thought.

His efforts at retrieval have been done for the sake of the renewal of the church. While George has excelled as a scholar, he is first and foremost a churchman. Through his study of the Reformers and other shapers of Christian history, George developed a deep appreciation for the role of the Word of God across the ages. He has insisted that Scripture must have a magisterial role in the life of the church while historical theology carries out a ministerial one. In so many ways, his work as scholar and administrator is an extension of his calling as a pastor-theologian and his conviction that theology is to be done in service to the church.

His years of service as a historical theologian have enabled him to see and interpret current squabbles by considering the bigger and broader picture of how Christians in the past have responded to similar challenges. At times he has assumed the role of polemicist as with the work on Islam noted earlier. His primary attention, however, has been as irenicist, seeking to bring people together and encouraging them toward reconciliation and renewal, always doing so from the standpoint of genuine biblical conviction. He has developed a well-earned reputation as a true statesman because he has looked for gospel-centered common ground, not because of any kind of convictionless approach to ecumenism. His life reflects his affirmation that the church is one, holy, catholic, and apostolic. One of his favorite hymns, "For All the Saints," a classic Christian expression, poetically portrays the theological commitments made known in the George's beliefs regarding the communion of the saints.

I personally have had the joy of calling Timothy George a close friend and co-laborer for more than thirty-five years. Over this period, I have observed his life and multi-faceted and wide-ranging work. In addition, I have carefully read many of his writings through the years. Nevertheless, I have learned even more about this influential historical theologian through the illuminating work of Chris Hanna. My appreciation for both Chris Hanna and Timothy George has certainly deepened in the process. It is a joy to recommend *Retrieval for the Sake of Renewal* and trust that many will find it to be beneficial, edifying, and instructive.

David S. Dockery
President, International Alliance for Christian Education
Distinguished Professor of Theology
Southwestern Baptist Theological Seminary

Acknowledgements

I AM FOREVER GRATEFUL for "the grace of the Lord Jesus Christ and the love of God and the fellowship of the Holy Spirit" (2 Cor 13:14).

Sara Adeli Hanna, you are the love of my life, and it is my greatest joy to be your husband. You always support and believe in me. I would not have succeeded in writing this book without your support and encouragement. During the writing of this work, we grieved the loss of our first child, Jude Argo Hanna, and we celebrated the birth of our second child, Christopher Beckham Hanna. You are an amazing wife and mother.

Steve Hanna, my father, I miss you so much. Cindy Hanna, my mother, I appreciate you reading my writing and encouraging me to do my best. My siblings, Andy and Lauren, I am thankful for your support. Kambiz Adeli, my father-in-law, you treat me like your son, and I am proud to be in your family. Bobby and Jeanette Ray, my maternal grandparents, you always support me. Mark and Ellen Hanna, my paternal grandparents, you showed me the value of education and lifelong learning.

Timothy George, I want to express my great esteem and sincere gratitude for you. Thank you for meeting with me and providing invaluable direction for this research. I am deeply grateful for what I have learned about historical theology from you and from those who have influenced you. To borrow imagery from C. S. Lewis, when I was a student at Beeson Divinity School your approach to historical theology was the wardrobe that I walked through to get to Narnia, an exciting new place where I discovered

Acknowledgements

the wonderful works of Augustine, Aquinas, Calvin, Luther, Wesley, and many others. I hope this book will chart the path to help others discover the same theological value in church history that I have learned from you.

Jason Duesing, your guidance was significant for me during my doctoral seminars and dissertation writing. I have benefited from your excellent teaching, engaging discussions, and the direction you provided for my writing and research. Thank you so much for your work as my professor and my dissertation supervisor.

My professors at Beeson Divinity School, thank you for teaching with excellence and encouraging me: Frank Thielman, Lyle Dorsett, Robert Smith, Gerald Bray, Piotr Malysz, Carl Beckwith, Thomas Fuller, Mark Gignilliat, Paul House, Kenneth Mathews, Osvaldo Padilla, David Parks, and Allen Ross. Mark DeVine, thank you for serving on my dissertation committee and meeting with me to share your insights and feedback. You inspired me to research Timothy George's understanding of historical theology.

My professors at Midwestern Baptist Theological Seminary, thank you for sharpening my research and writing skills: Thor Madsen, Jason Duesing, John Mark Yeats, Matthew Barrett, and Michael McMullen. I also appreciate the staff and resources of Midwestern Baptist Theological Seminary Library and the Samford University Library.

I am also grateful for the support of Chris Hodges, Mark Pettus, Beth Cunningham, Steve Blair, Layne Schranz, Gina Cox, Matthew Benson, and John Ball. It is my privilege to teach on the faculty of Highlands College and my honor to serve the members of Church of the Highlands with you.

1

Introduction

> My task is to convince you that there was someone between your grandmother and Jesus, and it matters.
>
> —TIMOTHY GEORGE

The Influence of Timothy George

AT THE END OF the 2019 academic year, Timothy George retired as the founding dean of Beeson Divinity School of Samford University in Birmingham, Alabama, completing thirty years of administration and teaching (1989–2019).[1] He has achieved a well-known reputation as a Reformation scholar and the contribution of his work in historical theology has been widely recognized by key figures in the Southern Baptist Convention (SBC) and beyond.[2]

A brief survey of what others from within and beyond George's denomination have said about him demonstrates his widespread influence in North American evangelicalism in the areas of theological education, local church ministry, denominational organizations, and engagement with Roman

---

1. Padilla, "Divinity School Founding Dean."
2. See "Timothy George," https://www.crossway.org/authors/timothy-george/. "His textbook *Theology of the Reformers* is the standard textbook on Reformation theology in many schools and seminaries."

Catholics. George's influence within the context of North American evangelicalism, Reformation studies, and theological education establishes the significance of researching his vision for an evangelical historical theology.

Why is Timothy George and his view of historical theology a worthy subject of this book? Timothy George is a Harvard-educated theologian from poverty-stricken Hell's Half Acre in Chattanooga, Tennessee. From 1978 until 1988, he taught church history and historical theology at the Southern Baptist Theological Seminary in Louisville, Kentucky. In 1989 he founded Beeson Divinity School of Samford University in Birmingham, Alabama, and now teaches as the Distinguished Professor of Divinity. He held leadership roles in the SBC and the Baptist World Alliance. He played a key role in the Evangelicals and Catholics Together dialogue. He served as a senior editor and executive editor for *Christianity Today*.

John Woodbridge, who is the research professor of church history and the history of Christian thought at Trinity Evangelical Divinity School, provided an excellent account of and praise for the work of Timothy George. He offered the following observation: "Today Timothy George is one of America's most respected church historians, theologians, and Christian educators. The influence of his marvelous ministry for Christ is extensive indeed."[3]

Influence in Theological Education Within the SBC

Timothy George has served in theological education and administration for over thirty years and has been respected by other leaders in theological education. An example from a Southern Baptist Seminary is Al Mohler, who is the president of the Southern Baptist Theological Seminary. He describes George as "a teacher of passion, a scholar of the first rank, a churchman of deep conviction, and a writer of great ability."[4] Mohler was one of George's students at Southern Seminary. He recalls, "When I arrived as a seminary student, now almost four decades ago, my own vocation as a pastor and theologian was encouraged and immeasurably deepened through the influence of one professor above all others. That professor was Timothy

---

3. Woodbridge, "Timothy George," 276. Woodbridge remarks, "George, a brilliant essayist, church historian, and theologian, has been one of the principal Evangelical participants in ECT. It is quite difficult to imagine the existence of the ECT enterprise without his significant irenic involvement." Woodbridge, "Timothy George," 263.

4. From Mohler's published endorsement for George, *Theology of the Reformers*.

Introduction

F. George. It was Timothy F. George who introduced me to the riches of Christian history."[5]

Professors from seminaries within the SBC recognize the contributions of George. David Allen is the former professor of preaching at Southwestern Baptist Theological Seminary. He commends George's writing: "I have long regarded Timothy George to reside at the apex of gifted writers in the Baptist world."[6] Malcolm Yarnell, the Research Professor of Systematic Theology, identified George as one of today's "prominent Baptist historians."[7]

Influence in Theological Education Beyond the SBC

David Dockery is the former president of Trinity International University.[8] He refers to George as "one of the premier historical theologians of our day."[9] Trinity University and its Evangelical Divinity School (TEDS) represent a good sample of evangelical and interdenominational scholarship outside of the SBC. Scott Manetsch, professor of church history at Trinity Evangelical Divinity School, states, "Timothy George's call for evangelical réssourcement—to retrieve Christian wisdom from the past for the sake of contemporary renewal—offers a particularly hopeful way forward."[10]

Kevin Vanhoozer, the research professor of systematic theology at TEDS, uses imagery[11] from Walt Whitman to express the respect and trust he has for George. Vanhoozer states, "Timothy George has for some years been the captain of the Good Ship Evangelical, and I have learned implicitly

---

5. Mohler, "Church and Pastor-Theologians," 29.

6. From Allen's published endorsement for George, *Theology of the Reformers*.

7. Yarnell, "Calvinism," 91. Yarnell commends George's work, *Theologians of the Baptist Tradition*, for making "a number of primary and secondary sources" available and providing a "fine collection." Yarnell, however, offers his critique of the work that "one could conclude that Calvinists were the only historically important Baptists."

8. See "David S. Dockery." Dockery is currently the "Distinguished Professor of Theology, Editor of the Southwestern Journal of Theology; Director of the Dockery Center for Global Evangelical Theology; Special Consultant to the President."

9. From Dockery's published endorsement for George, *Theology of the Reformers*.

10. Manetsch, "John Calvin," 178.

11. Vanhoozer, "Sola Scriptura, Tradition and Catholicity," 109. "O Captain! my Captain! our fearful trip is done, The ship has weather'd every rack, the prize we sought is won."

to trust his good judgment each time we set sail on a new dialogical doctrinal adventure."[12]

Influence in Local Church Ministry

One example of George's influence in local church ministry is his relationship with Mark Dever. Dever is the pastor of Capitol Hill Baptist Church in Washington, DC. He reflects on the important direction that George provided him. He explains, "It is in part because of Timothy George's friendship and kind encouragement that I declined an opportunity to teach in a seminary and have, instead, given the past twenty years to pastoring the Capitol Hill Baptist Church in Washington, DC."[13] He observed, "For Timothy, Bible truth and Christian life come together in the local church."[14] It is worth noting that George preached at Dever's Installation Service at Capitol Hill on September 25, 1994.[15] He titled his sermon, "The Responsibility of the Local Church," preaching on the Scripture passage 2 Cor 1:12–14.

Influence in Denominational Organizations

The extent of George's influence among denominational organizations inside the SBC can be evidenced by Thom Rainer, who is the former President & CEO of LifeWay Christian Resources. Rainer describes George as "the preeminent living Church historian."[16] Russell Moore, former President of the Ethics and Religious Liberty Commission (ELRC) of the SBC, comments on the significance of George's book on the Reformation when

---

12. Vanhoozer, "Sola Scriptura, Tradition and Catholicity," 109.

13. Dever, "Lose the Church," 46. Dever explains, "Timothy had been the supervisor of my ThM thesis in the mid-1980s and had become a close friend. Unlike many professors however, Timothy has never understood his own profession as the apex of Christian callings. He has a humble and profound joy in the pastoral office, and a respect and esteem for it often lacking in academics. And so, when others counseled against my accepting the pastorate of a largely elderly congregation in typical, inner-city decline, Timothy alone spoke to me of what wonderful things God might do there. He seemed to understand intuitively what I have been arguing in this chapter. For Timothy, Bible truth and Christian life come together in the local church."

14. Dever, "Lose the Church," 46.

15. George, "Responsibility of the Local Church." George has preached five times at Capitol Hill Baptist Church since Dever became its pastor.

16. From Rainer's published endorsement for George, *Theology of the Reformers*.

Introduction

he wrote, "Timothy George's *Theology of the Reformers* is my favorite book on the turbulent era of the Protestant Reformation."[17]

Influence with Roman Catholics

George's ecumenical influence can be evidenced by the observation of Roman Catholic Thomas G. Guarino, Professor of Systematic Theology of Seton Hall University. Guarino views George as a model of true ecumenism: "Timothy George is a model of that method and ecumenical posture. While fully committed to his Baptist heritage and to biblical truth, Dr. George has always been an ecumenist of the first rank: listening, seeking to understand, learning and, when necessary, disagreeing and offering alternatives."[18] George has defined and defended the importance of the Evangelicals and Catholics Together dialogue.[19]

The Central Question

This book will address the central question of Timothy George's understanding of historical theology in terms of its significance (chapter 1), biographical context (chapter 2), conceptual formation (chapter 3–5), and definition (chapter 6). First, why is Timothy George and his view of historical theology a worthy subject of this book? Second, what are the relevant details in Timothy George's life that help the reader better understand his background, family of origin, development, and formative years? Third, who are the key influencers that shaped his understanding of historical theology? Fourth, how does he define Christian doctrine and its historical orientation and development? Fifth, what are the characteristics that define his approach to historical theology? Answering these five questions should establish a strong framework for further studies of Timothy George, Christian doctrine, and the task of historical theology.

This work will offer the first book-length analysis of George's understanding of historical theology by describing and analyzing the key figures that shaped him. This book is the first study of the thought of Timothy George as an interpretation of George Huntston Williams, David Steinmetz,

---

17. From Moore's published endorsement for George, *Theology of the Reformers*.
18. Guarino, "Vatican II and 'Evangelicals and Catholics,'" 259.
19. See George, "Between the Pope and Billy Graham," 125–37.

and Jaroslav Pelikan. George has written more than twenty books and has served in both theological education and local church ministry; however, this work will be the first book devoted to George's approach to historical theology.

The Plan of This Book

This book will argue that Timothy George's perspective as a historical theologian is an interpretation of George Huntston Williams, Jaroslav Pelikan, and David Steinmetz. Therefore, this present study will employ the method of intellectual biography to explore these three personal influences upon George's historical and theological approach. This book seeks to study George's approach by placing him in the context of the professors that formed his perspective: George Huntston Williams (who modeled ecumenism, social activism, and church history as a theological discipline), David Steinmetz (who detailed the Reformers and pre-critical exegesis), and Jaroslav Pelikan (who surveyed the grand scope of the Christian tradition, Christian doctrine, and the Creeds). This book will argue that all three of these influences combine to inform George's intellectual approach to historical theology in his teaching, scholarship, and leadership.

Chapter 2, "Hell's Half Acre, Harvard, and Historical Theology: Timothy George (1950–)," will present an overview of George's early life, his Harvard Divinity School education, his teaching career at Southern Seminary, and the accomplishments of his work at Beeson Divinity School of Samford University. What are the relevant details in George's life that help the reader better understand his background, family of origin, development, and formative years? This chapter will present the relevant background information that provides a personal context to understand him. This chapter will identify and reflect on key developmental scenes and experiences in his formative years.

Chapter 3, "A Holy Calling, to Keep Truth Alive: George Huntston Williams (1914–2000)," will begin the focus on the influences on George's perspective of historical theology with George Huntston Williams. What are the components that make up Timothy George's understanding of historical theology? Who are the key persons and events that shaped George's understanding of Christian doctrine and the purpose of historical theology? This chapter will begin to address those questions by presenting a profile of George Huntston Williams. The profile will examine Williams's

Introduction

biographical and professional context, historical and theological approach, and key thoughts and contributions of ecumenism, social activism, and church history as a theological discipline.

Chapter 4, "The Quest to Free the Church from Amnesia: David Steinmetz (1936–2015)," will present a profile of David Steinmetz. The profile will examine Steinmetz's biographical and professional context, historical and theological approach, and key thoughts and contributions such as his work on the Reformers and argument for pre-critical exegesis. To take a case in point, George reflects on the link between his work as the general editor of the *Reformation Commentary on Scripture* and the work of David Steinmetz. He concludes, "The Reformation Commentary on Scripture . . . would not have been possible without the pioneering work of Steinmetz."[20] George refers to Steinmetz in four main categories: a Beloved Teacher, a Pioneering Scholar, a Respecter of the Text, and a Committed Churchman.[21]

Chapter 5, "Delighted by Doctrine: Jaroslav Pelikan (1923–2006)," will present a profile of Jaroslav Pelikan. The profile will examine Pelikan's biographical and professional context, historical and theological approach, and key thoughts and contributions to George's view of historical theology. Pelikan taught at Valparaiso University, Concordia Theological Seminary, the University of Chicago, and Yale University. George considered Pelikan the "best church historian America has ever produced."[22] He wrote about the grand scope of the Christian tradition. He operated from orthodoxy and tradition rather than the theological liberalism and the historical relativism of Adolf von Harnack.

Pelikan's work on the doctrinal content of the Christian tradition and creeds are significant in the perspective of George. He borrowed Pelikan's definition of Christian doctrine as what the "church of Jesus Christ has believed, taught, and confessed on the basis of the word of God."[23] He views Pelikan as a guide to the Grand Scope of the Christian Tradition, Christian doctrine, and the Creeds.

Chapter 6, "Evangelical Ecumenism: Timothy George's Understanding of Historical Theology," will bring together the influences of Williams, Steinmetz, and Pelikan, and will explore George's view and work in historical theology. How is a Southern Baptist Evangelical's perspective the result

---

20. George, "In Honor of David Steinmetz," para. 6.
21. George, "In Honor of David Steinmetz."
22. George, "Delighted by Doctrine," para. 1.
23. George, "Jesus on Safari," para. 1.

of the influences of a Harvard Professor who is a Unitarian, a Yale Professor who was a Lutheran and then an Eastern Orthodox, and a Duke Professor who is a United Methodist? This section will discuss George's understanding of the "hierarchy of ecclesial identity" and his approach of "ecumenism of conviction not accommodation" that lay the foundation for assimilating and developing a unique approach to historical theology.

Chapter 6 brings together the themes of previous chapters in an examination of the contemporary implications of George's historical theology. What implications are there for the church today based on George's views and practice of historical theology? What guidance and resources does this perspective offer the academic theologian and the pastor theologian?

This chapter will provide principles for practicing historical theology for the church with Timothy George as a model. This chapter will consider changes to current models of theological education curriculum by arguing for the inclusion, integration, and priority of historical theology in the theological curriculum. This chapter will outline implications for the academic theologian and the pastor theologian and bring the book to a close by offering key findings from George's view of historical theology through a summary of the main arguments presented throughout the book.

2
———

Hell's Half Acre, Harvard, and Historical Theology

Timothy George (1950–)

> To this day, I can think of nothing in ministry more exhilarating, apart from preaching the gospel, than helping to prepare God-called men and women for the service of the church of Jesus Christ.
>
> —TIMOTHY GEORGE

Introduction

THIS CHAPTER PRESENTS AN overview of George's early life and education in Chattanooga, Tennessee (1950–72), his Harvard Divinity School education in Cambridge, Massachusetts (1972–78), his teaching career at the Southern Baptist Theological Seminary in Louisville, Kentucky (1978–88), and the beginning of his work at Beeson Divinity School of Samford University in Birmingham, Alabama (1988–present). This chapter presents relevant background information that provides a personal context for understanding him. It also seeks to identify and reflect on key figures, developmental scenes, and experiences during his formative years.

The central question of this book, Timothy George's understanding of historical theology, has been established in terms of significance (chapter 1), and this chapter contributes to its biographical context (chapter 2) and introduces the key influencers that will be shown to shape his understanding of historical theology (chapters 3–5).

Chattanooga, Tennessee (1950–72)

Early Life

Timothy Francis George was born at Erlanger Hospital in Chattanooga, Tennessee, on January 9, 1950. He would face significant socioeconomic obstacles before he would become known as an "intellectual leader among Southern Baptist conservatives."[1] David Dockery describes George during his childhood as a "desperately poor kid from Chattanooga."[2]

Family Life

Sadly, George's parents were not capable of caring for him during his early years. His father was an abusive alcoholic, and his mother was a victim of spousal abuse and suffered from a debilitating illness. He remembers, "My father was an alcoholic, my mother had polio. Neither one of them were able to care for me or for my sister."[3] Dockery explains, "His father was an alcoholic who died in prison when George was twelve years old. By his own description, Timothy grew up in a dysfunctional family where his father violently abused him, his mother, and his sister."[4]

During his early life, Timothy lived apart from his younger sister Lynda. She was taken to a Baptist children's home in Cleveland, Tennessee, while Timothy was taken to live with his two great aunts, Mary Elizabeth George and Hattie Ann Nash. As George points out, "I was brought up in the care of these wonderful great-aunts, neither of whom could read or write, but they encouraged me to go to the library and do all kind of things."[5] George remembers their care, "[They] loved me and nurtured me through my early years, through at least the first grade, so I was brought up in a section of town that was not very wealthy."[6]

1. Wills, *Southern Baptist Seminary*, 511.
2. Dockery, "Timothy George," 3.
3. George, interview by Musgraves at Birmingham, AL, on August 18, 2014.
4. Dockery, "Timothy George," 3.
5. George, interview by Musgraves at Birmingham, AL, on August 18, 2014.
6. George, interview by Musgraves at Birmingham, AL, on August 18, 2014.

Hell's Half Acre, Harvard, and Historical Theology

Hell's Half Acre

The place where George grew up was known as "Hell's Half Acre between 23rd Street and Main Street."[7] Dockery describes this area as the inner city[8] and an "interracial neighborhood."[9] George explains how during the 1950s his childhood neighborhood in Tennessee was integrated even before the Civil Rights era because "both whites and blacks there were simply too poor to live anywhere else. I know what it is like to go to bed hungry and to go to school wearing raggedy clothes."[10] George further clarifies how his neighborhood was integrated not because of the presence of "uppity liberals trying to make a social statement but simply because none of us, neither whites nor African Americans, could afford to live anywhere else. I would have said that we were dirt poor, but we couldn't afford any dirt."[11]

The Public Library and Public School

The local public library played a crucial role in developing George's interests. He states, "Well, I remember one summer, I checked out 50 books, and I read them all. They were mostly biography, and I guess in a way, that's where my interest in history was born."[12] George's interest in history and especially biographies characterize his later career and writing.

The role of the local public school was also significant in George's development. He recounts, "Teachers took a special interest in me and encouraged me."[13] It was when one of his teachers gave him a class assignment in elementary school that he discovered he could speak in front of others and enjoyed it. He says, "That was about the same time I started preaching."[14] In other words, he views a positive connection between his public speaking experience in school and his interest in preaching from

---

7. George, interview by Musgraves at Birmingham, AL, on August 18, 2014.
8. Dockery, "Timothy George," 3.
9. Dockery, "Timothy George," 3.
10. George, "Journey into the Unknown," 70.
11. George, "Is Jesus a Baptist?," 89.
12. George, interview by Musgraves at Birmingham, AL, on August 18, 2014.
13. George, interview by Musgraves at Birmingham, AL, on August 18, 2014.
14. George, interview by Musgraves at Birmingham, AL, on August 18, 2014.

being "encouraged by the school system. I had wonderful teachers all the way through."[15]

As Dockery points out, "In his early years, George was blessed with outstanding teachers in elementary school through junior high school who advanced his love for learning, reading, books, poetry, and quality music."[16] His musical talents only went as far as playing the baritone horn in the junior high school band. His high school English teacher, Lucile Johnson, "made poetry come alive" for him.[17] While his local library and the local school were instrumental in his formation, nothing could have been more formative than his local church and its lasting impact on him.

Conversion

Growing up, Timothy George attended a "country church in the city."[18] His great-aunts took him to the nearby Baptist church every Sunday. He describes the worship experience as "expressive, the prayers fervent, and the love palpable."[19] It was in this small, vibrant church that he first learned "John 3:16 and the chorus 'Jesus loves me, this I know, for the Bible tells me so.'"[20] He says, "Sunday school was a big deal, and so was the preaching. In that church, I first connected with one of the Bible's great journey stories: Abraham and Sarah's pilgrimage from an old home to a new one, from an old country to a different one (Heb. 11:8–16)."[21]

In recounting his conversion experience, George says, "Through the loving nurture I received from that congregation, I confessed my personal

---

15. George, interview by Musgraves at Birmingham, AL, on August 18, 2014.

16. Dockery, "Timothy George," 3.

17. See Bracey, "Interview with Timothy George." George on his love for music: "But I do love music and listen to it often, especially on trips and while doing my daily walks. Johann Sebastian Bach is my favorite by far. No one else even comes close, though Mozart tries. But I also love country music, especially bluegrass. Give me a root beer and a couple of Louvin Brothers CDs, and I'm just fine!" George on his love for poetry: "Poetry has an evocative power that speaks to the heart. Our hymnals contain some of the greatest Christian poems ever written. I love poetry of all kinds. Some of my favorites are T. S. Eliot, W. H. Auden, Christina Rossetti, Emily Dickenson, John Donne, George Herbert, and the contemporary poet Mary Oliver."

18. George, "Is Jesus a Baptist?," 89.

19. George, "Journey into the Unknown," 72.

20. George, "Journey into the Unknown," 72.

21. George, "Journey into the Unknown," 72.

faith in Jesus as Savior and Lord of my life. I was then baptized in the name of the Father, the Son, and the Holy Spirit."[22] He speaks of how he was baptized "by Dr. Lee Roberson, a wonderful independent Baptist pastor. I imbibed the best of that tradition along with a kind of raw, rural, no-holds-barred Southern Baptist fundamentalism."[23]

George expresses gratitude for "those dear saints who introduced me to Jesus Christ."[24] He recognizes the strengths and weaknesses of his church setting and this stage of his spiritual formation. The strengths consisted of George learning to love God's Word and "to take seriously the evangelistic mission of the church."[25]

George, however, admits that there were "some significant gaps in my spiritual upbringing,"[26] for instance, a lack of "appreciation for the Word of God across the ages."[27] Emphasizing the importance of how the word of God has been understood and appreciated across the ages will characterize his later ministry and writing. He captures the lack of appreciation in the following way, "We sort of had the idea that we had received our faith from grandma or Uncle Robert, and that they had received theirs directly from Jesus. We were not much aware of anything in between."[28]

Learning to be a Theologian

While Timothy George was raised in a Baptist church, most of his extended family were members of the Church of Jesus Christ of Latter-Day Saints (LDS), also known as Mormons. One family member, in particular, who was the only present male role model in George's life, was his Uncle Willie. George describes him as a "dyed-in-the-wool Mormon."[29]

George's engagement with Mormonism had a positive outcome. George believes that he "learned to be a theologian arguing with him and the Mormon missionaries who tried to convert me when I was quite young,

---

22. George, "Why I Am an Evangelical," 108.
23. Barrett, "Reading Scripture with the Reformers," 68.
24. Barrett, "Reading Scripture with the Reformers," 68.
25. Barrett, "Reading Scripture with the Reformers," 68.
26. Barrett, "Reading Scripture with the Reformers," 68.
27. George, interview by Musgraves at Birmingham, AL, on August 18, 2014.
28. George, interview by Musgraves at Birmingham, AL, on August 18, 2014.
29. George, interview by Musgraves at Birmingham, AL, on August 18, 2014.

to the Mormon faith."[30] George undertook a process of understanding and comparing doctrine, and more importantly, weighing it carefully with his view and interpretation of the Bible.

He says, "I had to learn all of that stuff; read the Bible and argue about the Bible, but Aunt Mary was a Baptist. She'd never become a Mormon, and so she took me to the Boulevard Baptist Church in Chattanooga. That was my early Christian religious training."[31]

George was the first person in his family to receive a college education.[32] While many of his relatives were not able to "read or write, they could certainly talk, think, and argue."[33] He says, "I am sure I received my calling as a theologian from endless hours of arguing with my Uncle Willie over the truth claims of Mormonism. Once I straightened him out, I took on the Unitarians down the street and the Roman Catholics across town."[34]

Calling

Timothy George's understanding of his calling is not primarily that of an administrator, scholar, or teacher. Dockery explains, "To this day, George interprets his call to ministry not as leader, teacher, scholar, or theologian, but as preacher of the gospel growing out on his reading of Romans 10 while still a young boy."[35]

George provides an account of his calling experience: "August 6th, 1961, I give you a specific date because I remember that date."[36] He continues, "I had gone to church—we were going to a church at that time, not Boulevard, but another church, very Baptist kind of church, but there was something, an organization called the Woman's Missionary Union. . . . My mother was a part of that, and so she brought home a magazine called the Royal Service."[37]

Always the avid reader, George started reading the "devotional or Bible study in the Royal Service, based on Romans chapter 10: 'How beautiful are

30. George, interview by Musgraves at Birmingham, AL, on August 18, 2014.
31. George, interview by Musgraves at Birmingham, AL, on August 18, 2014.
32. George, interview by Musgraves at Birmingham, AL, on August 18, 2014.
33. George, interview by Musgraves at Birmingham, AL, on August 18, 2014.
34. George, "Is Jesus a Baptist?," 89.
35. Dockery, "Timothy George," 3.
36. George, interview by Musgraves at Birmingham, AL, on August 18, 2014.
37. George, interview by Musgraves at Birmingham, AL, on August 18, 2014.

the feet of those who preach the Gospel.'"[38] He describes how while reading this passage of Scripture, God "gripped my heart and I felt that that was meant for me, that I was to be the one to go over the hills and the mountains preaching the Gospel."[39]

When George received his calling to preach, he was in an environment in which, he says, "No one ever told me that you had to go to college or seminary and get ordained and certificated and all that to be a preacher."[40] Instead, he immediately began preaching. He remembers preaching on "youth Sundays, youth days, I told my pastor, he'd give me opportunities to preach, so that's how it started."[41]

Early Ministry

Timothy George became a youth evangelist. At the young age of eleven, he was eager to begin his preaching ministry. He says, "Well, I wanted to preach so badly, that sometimes I would preach at recess, that is the little time between class when you'd go out and play."[42]

Though his classmates were not eager to hear a sermon during their play time, George was determined that they hear his preaching. He says, "I would collar students; I used to be a bully, you can hardly tell that by looking at my gentle countenance now, but I'd say, 'You'd better come over and listen to me,' and I'd actually preach a sermon to the kids on recess."[43]

George admits, "Another thing I did, I would do when I would be chopping wood sometimes, is I would string up bottles along the sill, I'd preach to Coke bottles and stuff like that. Once I had a bird's funeral, I remember. This was when I was early starting out, but then I graduated to youth revivals."[44]

Youth revivals were a common practice in the Baptist tradition in the 1960s. George remembers, "That's what Baptist people like me did in those days. I was a Baptist preacher boy, and I did a lot of youth revivals, all the way through high school. My last senior year in high school, I did 28 youth

---

38. George, interview by Musgraves at Birmingham, AL, on August 18, 2014.
39. George, interview by Musgraves at Birmingham, AL, on August 18, 2014.
40. George, interview by Musgraves at Birmingham, AL, on August 18, 2014.
41. George, interview by Musgraves at Birmingham, AL, on August 18, 2014.
42. George, interview by Musgraves at Birmingham, AL, on August 18, 2014.
43. George, interview by Musgraves at Birmingham, AL, on August 18, 2014.
44. George, interview by Musgraves at Birmingham, AL, on August 18, 2014.

revivals, so almost every other week, and loved it all. Somehow, I managed to graduate, I don't see how now."[45]

The peak of George's "youth evangelism career"[46] was preaching in Lynchburg, Virginia, at Thomas Road Baptist Church led by Jerry Falwell.[47] George recalls that his pastor, Dr. J. Ralph McIntyre, at Brainerd Baptist Church in Chattanooga, Tennessee was the one who ordained him "to the gospel ministry."[48]

One of George's early mentors was Sam D. Sharp. Sharp was a "fiery evangelist."[49] He says that Sharp "took me under his wing and, though he had had no opportunity to receive a formal education himself, said to me: 'Timothy, read all you can, learn all you can, and don't be afraid of ideas. You can believe the tomb is empty without your head having to be!'"[50] Guidance and encouragement from figures like Sam Sharp, his great aunts, and his school teachers inspired George to be the first person in his family to go to college.

Undergraduate Studies

Timothy George first engaged with the Reformation seriously through his study of history.[51] He majored in history at the University of Tennessee-Chattanooga, where he learned from "superb teachers, including Dr. William J. Wright, a student of Harold Grimm."[52] George says, "Bill Wright and other teachers at UTC made history, and especially the era of the Reformation, come alive for me."[53]

Roland H. Bainton's work, *Here I Stand*, was one of the books that inspired George's interest in the Reformation.[54] He says, "I first read it as an undergraduate, and it hooked me on the Reformation. *Here I Stand* tells the story of Luther as it has never been told before or since. Doctor

45. George, interview by Musgraves at Birmingham, AL, on August 18, 2014.
46. George, "Is Jesus a Baptist?," 90.
47. George, "Is Jesus a Baptist?," 90.
48. George, *Amazing Grace*, 53.
49. George, "Is Jesus a Baptist?," 90.
50. George, "Is Jesus a Baptist?," 90–91.
51. George, "Is Jesus a Baptist?," 90–91.
52. George, "Is Jesus a Baptist?," 90–91.
53. Barrett, "Reading Scripture with the Reformers," 68.
54. Bainton, *Here I Stand*.

Martinus almost steps off every page, a real human being beset by guilt but saved by grace."[55]

Marriage

Timothy George's early ministry of evangelistic preaching took him to many churches. During this time, he met Denise Wyse at Flintstone Baptist Church. Flintstone is located in Northwest Georgia in the foothills of Lookout Mountain close to Chattanooga.

Dockery recounts, "While preaching at the Flintstone Baptist Church as an older teenager, he was introduced to and captivated by the lovely Denise Wyse. At the young ages of twenty and nineteen respectively, Timothy and Denise were married at the Flintstone Church in Chickamauga, GA."[56] The young married couple honeymooned in Atlanta, Georgia.

During the honeymoon, Timothy "found a discount bookstore where he bought all of Calvin's commentaries."[57] Dockery views George's honeymoon purchase, which can be understood in historical, theological, and biblical categories, as "an adumbration of the theological and scholarly interests that would characterize the rest of his life."[58]

Cambridge, Massachusetts (1972–78)

George's decision about where to receive his theological education was a difficult one. He remembers how he "struggled to decide which seminary to attend."[59] He faced denominational pressure and tensions. He describes the denominational pressure that he experienced when he wrote: "As a dyed-in-the-wool Southern Baptist preacher boy, everyone assumed I would choose one of our six denominational seminaries."[60]

At the same time, George was confronted with denominational tensions. He refers to how other local church leaders expressed concerns about liberalism in the seminaries when he said, "In the conservative Baptist

---

55. George, "My Top Five Classics," para. 2.
56. Dockery, "Timothy George," 3.
57. Dockery, "Timothy George," 3.
58. Dockery, "Timothy George," 3.
59. George, "Journey into the Unknown," 72.
60. George, "Journey into the Unknown," 72.

circles in which I had grown up around Chattanooga, Southern was regarded as far too 'liberal.'"[61] He was urged by those closest to him to consider going to either the New Orleans Baptist Theological Seminary or the Southwestern Baptist Theological Seminary.

He was directed to those schools, he said, by the "pastors I knew and trusted"[62] because those places were presented as "more biblical and evangelistic schools."[63] He was open to attending a denominational school. He visited one of the seminaries with his wife and took the time to meet with its professors.[64]

George, however, had other influences and priorities beyond these denominational pressures and tensions. He said, "I had some teachers at UTC whom I respected [who] said, 'You ought to think about going outside your region, outside your denomination.'"[65] He overcame the denominational pressure and tension in part by his educational influences and priorities.

He started to consider the possibility of studying at Harvard Divinity School. He explains, "I was very interested in studying history and studying the Reformation in particular, and there was a book I had read by George Huntston Williams, a great, great historian, church historian, who taught at Harvard. And I said, 'Wow, it would be great to study with this man.'"[66]

More important than George's educational priorities was his commitment to preach the gospel and continue his work as a pastor. While still in school, he became the pastor at Fellowship Baptist Church in Chickamauga, Georgia.

George wrote to the Home Mission Board of the Southern Baptist Convention about his interest in studying at Harvard Divinity School and his desire to continue his pastoral ministry.[67] He asked, "Is there anything I can do in mission work up there?"[68] They replied and asked him to consider becoming the pastor of First Baptist Church in Chelsea, Massachusetts, while he did his studies at Harvard. He became their pastor and received $300 a month from the Home Mission Board. He viewed this ministry

61. George, "*SBJT* Forum," 110.
62. George, "*SBJT* Forum," 110.
63. George, "*SBJT* Forum," 110.
64. George, "Journey into the Unknown," 72.
65. George, interview by Musgraves at Birmingham, AL, on August 18, 2014.
66. George, interview by Musgraves at Birmingham, AL, on August 18, 2014.
67. This SBC organization is now known as the North American Mission Board.
68. George, interview by Musgraves at Birmingham, AL, on August 18, 2014.

Hell's Half Acre, Harvard, and Historical Theology

opportunity as "an answer to prayer and a confirmation that's where I should go."[69] He was also awarded the Dora Maclellan Brown Ministry Scholarship, which helped students from the greater Chattanooga area afford graduate level theological education in their preparation for ministry.[70]

With this confirmation and after a period of careful reflection and discussion with Denise, George decided to attend Harvard Divinity School for his ministry training and theological education.[71] He tells of how he was "led to Harvard Divinity School, where I had the privilege of working with the great church historian, George Huntston Williams."[72] He wrote his dissertation, "The Role of John Robinson in the English Separatist Tradition," under Williams's supervision.[73]

During their time at Harvard, George and Denise "learned trust and vulnerability the hard way."[74] In relational and geographic terms, the young married couple was far away from their friends and family for the first time. At times their sense of security was challenged. George comments, "I will never forget that empty feeling in my stomach when I came out of class one day to discover that my car had been stolen. Our house and the adjacent church building were broken into on five separate occasions, our few valuable items stolen."[75] Culturally, even small things reinforced how far away from home they were. For example, Timothy and Denise struggled to "find grits in a Boston grocery store!"[76]

When George arrived at Harvard to begin his studies, he considered "the idea of pursuing doctoral studies in New Testament and early Christian origins."[77] While doing his graduate studies in historical and modern theology, however, he started to "see that one could not really leapfrog over the Reformation to recover an unmediated, primitivist kind of Christianity."[78] Instead, he was convinced that any serious student of Christian theology

---

69. George, interview by Musgraves at Birmingham, AL, on August 18, 2014.

70. See "Dr. Timothy George of Samford presents C.S. Lewis Lecture," and "Dora Maclellan Brown Ministry Scholarship Program."

71. George, "Journey into the Unknown," 72.

72. George, "*SBJT* Forum," 110.

73. "Summaries of Doctoral Dissertations," 315–22.

74. George, "Journey into the Unknown," 73.

75. George, "Journey into the Unknown," 73.

76. George, "Journey into the Unknown," 73.

77. George, "Journey into the Unknown," 73.

78. George, "Journey into the Unknown," 73.

"must come to grips with what happened theologically as well as historically during the great seismic divide of Western Christianity in the great sixteenth century."[79]

Therefore, for George, the study of the Reformation was about more than the Reformation. He explains, "Thus my interest in the Reformation was always in service to a wider concern, namely, to understand the reformers as they saw themselves: faithful servants of Jesus Christ in the one, holy, catholic, and apostolic church."[80] George was able to study with "great scholars of the Reformation, including David Steinmetz, Heiko Oberman, and George Huntston Williams. They all inspired me to dig deeply into Reformation theology."[81]

As a student at Harvard Divinity School in the 1970s, Timothy George encountered two drastically different approaches to studying Christianity. These approaches were opposite sides of the spectrum in understanding the intersection of theological and historical study. Harvey Cox and George Huntston Williams embodied these approaches. Critical and constructive interactions with these professors shaped not only George's time as a student at Harvard but also his perspective of historical theology.

George recalls, "When I arrived at Harvard Divinity School in the 1970s, I met Harvey Cox, like me a former Baptist youth evangelist. Cox was then in his post-Secular City, pre-postmodern phase and was much enamored with Buddhism and spiritualities of the East."[82]

George referenced Harvey Cox's research interests that resulted in the 1977 work by Cox entitled *Turning East*, while George was still a student at Harvard Divinity School. In this work Cox proposed the principle of genealogical selectivity. Cox's proposed principle was an approach to studying religion and, in this case, Christianity. He argued, "As late twentieth-century Christians trying to work out a viable spirituality, there are two principal historical sources to which we should look."[83] He pointed to "the earliest period of our history and the most recent, the first Christian generations and the generation just before us."[84]

---

79. Wax, "Theology of the Reformers."
80. Wax, "Theology of the Reformers."
81. Barrett, "Reading Scripture with the Reformers," 68.
82. George, *Reading Scripture with the Reformers*, 22.
83. Cox, *Turning East*, 157.
84. Cox, *Turning East*, 157.

Cox warned that "the ransacking of other periods for help in working out a contemporary spirituality soon becomes either antiquarian or downright misleading."[85] Thus, Cox undermined the value of studying different periods throughout church history for today. Cox claimed that the long period of Christian history should be viewed more "as a cautionary tale than a treasure house of available inspiration."[86] As a student, George rejected Cox's position and instead embraced the trajectory of another approach, which he would follow throughout his career in the study of Christianity.

George Huntston Williams

George Huntston Williams exemplified an approach far superior than Harvey Cox for studying Christianity. Williams positively shaped Timothy George's approach to church history and historical theology. George writes of Williams, saying, "He is one of three remarkable scholars who profoundly shaped my understanding of the church and its history."[87] He explains in what way his understanding was shaped when he writes, "During my seven years of graduate and postgraduate study at Harvard University, George Williams taught me to approach church history as a theological discipline and to understand the church as the body of Christ extended throughout time as well as space."[88] He elaborates, "I was trained in this approach by my great mentor at Harvard, George Huntston Williams. He taught us to seek connections and discern patterns—theological and historical—in every event or person or period we studied."[89]

George dedicated his first major work, *Theology of the Reformers*, to Williams. The dedication reveals at least three aspects in which George appreciated and benefited from him. The three aspects are his personal connection, professional admiration, and practical development. Personally, George relates to him as "Professor Williams, my mentor, and friend, who was a continuing source of encouragement and inspiration during seven years of graduate and postgraduate study at the Harvard Divinity School."[90] Professionally, George regards him as "One of the premier church historians

---

85. Cox, *Turning East*, 157.
86. Cox, *Turning East*, 159.
87. George, *Theology of the Reformers*, 4.
88. George, *Theology of the Reformers*, 4.
89. Wax, "Reformation Theology or Theologies?," para. 4.
90. George, *Theology of the Reformers*, 7.

of the twentieth century."[91] Practically, George looked to him as an example. He says, "Professor Williams modeled for me the two qualities required of anyone who aspires to the vocation of what Cotton Mather once called 'the Lord's remembrancer': a critical reverence for the Christian tradition in all of its varied modalities, and a sense of membership in the church universal, the body of Christ extended throughout time as well as space."[92]

David Steinmetz

Timothy George met David Steinmetz when Steinmetz was a visiting professor at Harvard. He says of Steinmetz, "I took his class on 'Calvin and the Reformed Tradition'. . . . Steinmetz also served on my doctoral examination committee."[93]

George admired Steinmetz as a leader in the classroom: "He was the best classroom teacher I have ever had. He was not only brilliant but also passionate and insightful."[94] George explains, "He never lost sight of the larger context of the texts and traditions he was so adept at bringing to life. I shall never forget his early morning lectures in Andover Hall, as he presented Calvin's life and thought like a great actor commanding the stage."[95]

George remembers his "lively lectures—replete with chalk-drawn diagrams on the blackboard, lively interrogations of 16th-century texts, and dramatic enactments of Reformation debates. You felt like you were there with Luther and Zwingli at Marburg, with Calvin and Bolsec in Geneva."[96]

Steinmetz also agreed with Williams about the purpose of "church history as a theological discipline."[97] He clarifies that this approach enables the church to have a "more universal and self-critical perspective within which to make responsible theological and pastoral decisions in the present."[98]

Steinmetz also addressed Harvey Cox's accusations that church history is antiquarian and a misleading direction when he wrote, "The invitation

---

91. George, *Theology of the Reformers*, 7.
92. George, *Theology of the Reformers*, 7.
93. George, "Remembering David Steinmetz's Quest," para. 3.
94. George, "Remembering David Steinmetz's Quest," para. 4.
95. George, "Remembering David Steinmetz's Quest," para. 4.
96. George, "Remembering David Steinmetz's Quest," para. 4.
97. Steinmetz, *Taking the Long View*, 143.
98. Steinmetz, *Taking the Long View*, 143.

to study the history of the church is not an irrelevant call to forsake the mission of the church and to lose oneself in a past no longer recoverable."[99] He not only clarified what historical theology is not but also what it is, when he said, "It is, rather, a call to abandon peripheral matters, to put an end to aimless meanderings and nervous activism, to learn once again who we are and to whom we belong. Only when we have regained our identity from the past can we undertake our mission in the present."[100]

Jaroslav Pelikan

Timothy George claims, "I never had Jaroslav Pelikan as a classroom teacher, but I was one of his students, as everyone seriously interested in Christian history has to be."[101] He recalls, "As a young student of historical theology, I once determined to read everything Pelikan had written. It is a daunting task, let me assure you: A 1995 bibliography of his works, which does not include his last prolific decade, runs to some 50 printed pages."[102]

George confronts the notion that the history of Christianity is irrelevant and insignificant by saying, "History is not just about dead people and stuff from the past. History shapes our consciousness today; it is part of who we are."[103] He gained this appreciation of the Christian past because he was "privileged to study with some of the greatest Christian historians of the twentieth century, including my mentor at Harvard, George Huntston Williams, the great Reformation historian Heiko O. Oberman, and David Steinmetz at Duke. Jaroslav Pelikan also had a great influence on the way I understand and practice historical theology."[104]

George argues that each of these scholars were united in their urgent and meaningful task when he says, "In a profound way, all of these great scholars shared a common mission: 'They were committed to keeping truth alive as a holy calling.' The heresy of contemporaneity is one of the greatest

---

99. Steinmetz, *Taking the Long View*, 143.
100. Steinmetz, *Taking the Long View*, 146.
101. George, "Delighted by Doctrine," 205.
102. George, "Delighted by Doctrine," 205. See Hotchkiss for a recent list of Pelikan's works, "Bibliography of Jaroslav Pelikan," 185–231.
103. Bracey, "Interview with Timothy George," para. 5.
104. Bracey, "Interview with Timothy George," para. 5.

dangers faced by today's church. A solid knowledge of church history is an antidote to that dead-end alley."[105]

Historical Theology: Keeping Truth Alive

George would soon join Williams, Steinmetz, and Pelikan as a partner in the mission to keep truth alive through his role as a professor. Although he says, "I didn't go to Harvard to become a teacher. I went to Harvard because I was a pastor."[106] He explains, "I wanted to be the best trained pastor I could be and I stayed on to do a doctoral degree for the same reason, but in the course of that, you know, I began to think about teaching possibilities and folks came to me and said, 'What do you think about teaching here or there?'"[107]

During the last years of George's doctoral studies, three theological schools were in contact with him about teaching jobs: Rüschlikon Theological Seminary in Zurich, Switzerland, Southeastern Baptist Theological Seminary in Wake Forest, North Carolina, and the Southern Baptist Theological Seminary in Louisville, Kentucky. He chose Southern for its educational reputation and recognition, his relational connections there, and their financial generosity.

First, George admired the educational rigor and resources at Southern. He said the school "was the best known, and I think at that time, maybe not the largest, but one of the best libraries and academic reputations, anyway, and that attracted me."[108] Second, he had personal connections already at Southern, like his friend Bill Leonard. Leonard had graduated from Boston University four years before he did from Harvard. Leonard was already teaching at Southern and encouraged him to come. Third, he appreciated their financial generosity. He remembers, "Southern was willing to hire me, essentially two years before I finished my degree, give me a contract on full salary at Harvard for that last year. . . . I actually joined the faculty in '78 and moved in '79 to Louisville."[109]

---

105. Bracey, "Interview with Timothy George," para. 7.
106. George, interview by Musgraves at Birmingham, AL, on August 18, 2014.
107. George, interview by Musgraves at Birmingham, AL, on August 18, 2014.
108. George, interview by Musgraves at Birmingham, AL, on August 18, 2014.
109. George, interview by Musgraves at Birmingham, AL, on August 18, 2014.

Hell's Half Acre, Harvard, and Historical Theology

Louisville, Kentucky (1978–88)

In 1978 George joined the faculty of the Southern Baptist Theological Seminary in Louisville, Kentucky, where he taught for the next ten years.[110] During his faculty interview, he attempted to be transparent about his theological convictions: "I wanted to lay all of my cards on the table, so to speak, and confessed that I was an inerrantist, a Calvinist, and a premillennialist. This brought some amusement to the group, and one person remarked that Southern had hired no one with those views for at least 100 years!"[111] He became known for his commitment to the authority of the Bible.[112] George explains, "I clearly understood myself to be one of the more conservative members of the faculty. That was clear from day one, but I didn't feel any particular discrimination."[113] He recalls, "Duke McCall was the president when I joined the faculty, and Roy Honeycutt was the dean. My friend Bill Leonard was already a member of the faculty and encouraged me to join him there."[114]

Teaching

Timothy George says, "It was at Southern that I learned to teach and learned to love teaching."[115] He remembers "Cave Hill Cemetery became a special place for meditation and prayer, and I often gave lectures to my students around the graves of Boyce, Broadus, Robertson, Mullins, and other leaders of the seminary who lie buried there."[116] He explains, "I found that students knew little, if anything, about those pioneers of the past, and I wanted to encourage a program of réssourcement—not a return to 'the good old days'

---

110. Wills, *Southern Baptist Seminary, 1859–2009*, 478.

111. George, "*SBJT* Forum," 111.

112. See "Contested Ground": "At Southern, professors Timothy George, Lewis Drummond, and David Dockery defended the inerrancy of the Bible, but the vast majority of the faculty rejected it and advanced liberal views in many areas of theology and ethics, as did the majority of the faculties at the other Southern Baptist seminaries" (para. 2).

113. George, interview by Musgraves at Birmingham, AL, on August 18, 2014.

114. George, "*SBJT* Forum," 111.

115. George, "*SBJT* Forum," 111.

116. George, "*SBJT* Forum," 111. Dockery comments, "Cave Hill Cemetery in Louisville, KY is the burial site for numerous shapers of Southern Baptist life including: James P. Boyce, John A. Broadus, Basil Manly, Jr., A. T. Robertson, E. Y. Mullins, and others." See Dockery, "Timothy George," 17.

but an appropriation of the warranted wisdom and spiritual insight they can offer to the church today."[117]

When George joined the Southern faculty, he had the unique assignment of being a part of the church history department as well as the theology department. He said, "Historical theology had not been pursued in a serious way since the departure of James Leo Garrett some years before. The effort to revive this discipline led to some tension, and one colleague suggested that I stick to the Reformation (in a narrow sense) and leave the history of doctrine alone."[118] Al Mohler still remembers George's opening statement for his church history class: "My task in this class is to convince you that there was someone between your grandmother and Jesus and that it matters."[119] George gave a chapel address presenting his approach to historical theology titled, "Dogma beyond Anathema: Historical Theology in the Service of the Church."[120]

Teaching students, who were eager to learn and be used by God in ministry, became the highlight of George's ten years at Southern. He says, "I was privileged to teach a cadre of superb students, highly motivated and eager to learn. Mark Dever, Mark DeVine, Al Mohler, Thom Rainer, Bruce Beck, Tim McCoy, Elizabeth Newman, Barry Harvey, Paul House, and Brent Walker are among the students I taught."[121] He says, "I rejoice in all that God continues to do through their life and witness."[122] These students and many more are the reasons that George says, "To this day, I can think of nothing in ministry more exhilarating, apart from preaching the gospel, than helping to prepare God-called men and women for the service of the church of Jesus Christ."[123]

Writing

The first ten years of Timothy George's teaching career culminates with him writing *Theology of the Reformers*, much of the writing taking place on a

---

117. George, "*SBJT* Forum," 111.

118. George, "*SBJT* Forum," 111.

119. See "Timothy George," http://archives.sbts.edu/the-history-of-the-sbts/our-professors/timothy-george/.

120. George, "Dogma beyond Anathema," 703.

121. George, "*SBJT* Forum," 111.

122. George, "*SBJT* Forum," 111.

123. George, "*SBJT* Forum," 111.

sabbatical in Zurich, Switzerland.[124] George's purpose in the book is to establish the religious climate of the Reformation period and take seriously the theological self-understanding of five major reformers. Dockery explains the significant impact of this work in the overall trajectory of George's career as a theologian. He writes, "George established himself as a premier Reformation scholar with the publication of the highly-praised *Theology of the Reformers* (1988), a work that guided readers through the thought of Martin Luther, John Calvin, Huldrych Zwingli, and Menno Simons."[125]

In this work, George addresses three perspectives in Reformation studies that are key considerations in Reformation scholarship. First, he addresses the problem of periodization. The challenge is how to understand the Reformation as a part of the medieval era or the modern era and its relationship with the themes of the Renaissance. The problem exists because the Reformation is related to both eras, medieval and modern. He argues that the resolution to the problem of periodization is to place the Reformation as a transition from the medieval period to the modern period.

Second, George surveys the sociological approach to the Reformation that attempts to understand the event through political, social, and economic means. For example, he proposes that the success of the Reformation in Germany, the failure of it in France, and the lack of any progress in Spain can all be tied to the political history of each nation-state. Socially, the Reformation can be examined by understanding the impact of urbanization, change in family structures, and the development of the printing press. Economically, the Reformation is affected by the conquest of gold, the breakdown of the feudal land system, and the emergence of capitalism.

Third, George introduces a position that approaches the Reformation from the perspective of ecumenical historiography. Notably, he mentions Joseph Lortz, a Roman Catholic scholar. Lortz wrote a two-volume study of the Reformation, which gives a critical but overall positive assessment of Martin Luther's contribution. Lortz ignited a whole line of Catholic scholars who became more appreciative of the writings and themes of the Protestant Reformation while remaining critical of its outcome.

---

124. George, *Theology of the Reformers*. See Hansen, "Timothy George and the Leadership That Lifts." Hansen states, "I don't know of any better introduction to what the major 16th-century reformers taught and believed. The fact that it was published by B&H for the Southern Baptist Convention is significant. Recovering the reformers' theology prepared a generation for the SBC's conservative resurgence of the 1980s and 1990s and then inspired the growth of Reformed theology in the SBC during the 2000s and 2010s."

125. Dockery, "Timothy George," 5.

Retrieval for the Sake of Renewal

George's perspective of the Reformation, as investigated in his work, was a *religious initiative*. He borrows this term and historiographical approach from John T. McNeill. He argues that the primary concern of the Reformation is not economic, social, or political. Instead, the Reformation's primary concern is theological. His aim in the book is to establish the religious climate of the period and carefully listen to the theological self-understanding of five major reformers. *Theology of the Reformers* is a significant achievement.[126] This ecumenical historiography carefully investigates and listens to the self-understanding of four major reformers: Martin Luther, Huldrych Zwingli, John Calvin, and Menno Simons. The second edition, published in 2013, includes William Tyndale.

Each chapter of *Theology of the Reformers* gives brief, detailed biographical information about each major reformer. George introduces readers to the key historical events that influenced the reformer and the theological contributions made by each. Each chapter ends with an extensive bibliography that enables the reader to continue learning about the person, history, or theology in question. His work is a vital contribution to understanding the Reformation period, its pivotal events, key figures, and theology.

During the 1980s, the Southern Baptist Convention and the Southern Baptist Theological Seminary experienced a time of conflict and transition, which George refers to this period as a "a major upheaval and reorientation, a time of turmoil and schism known to many of its participants simply as The Controversy."[127] Since the 1950s, the SBTS experienced an identity crisis evidenced by the struggle between members of the faculty and the denomination's churches about the purpose of the seminary.[128]

The churches desired for the seminary to be theologically orthodox and prioritize the congregational and ministerial needs of the denomination.[129] Certain members of the faculty, however, wanted the seminary to champion intellectual freedom even at the expense of theological fidelity. The school was at a pivotal intersection in the 1980s. Albert Mohler's

---

126. See "Timothy George," https://www.crossway.org/authors/timothy-george/. "His textbook *Theology of the Reformers* is the standard textbook on Reformation theology in many schools and seminaries."

127. George, "Southern Baptist Ghosts," 17–24.

128. Wills, *Southern Baptist Seminary, 1859–2009*, 358. Wills observes, "The fundamental divide in the faculty concerned the purpose and character of a theological seminary."

129. Wills, *Southern Baptist Seminary, 1859–2009*, 357. Wills states, "For many pastors and churches, the characteristic most greatly desired was orthodoxy."

presidency sought to embrace orthodoxy and provide excellent scholarship in service to the churches of the denomination.

George remembers the SBC conflict during his time at SBTS as "a raging controversy in the SBC and that just created some tense situations that involved me kind of on a periphery."[130] He said about the controversy, "That was certainly not a factor in why I left Southern to come to start Beeson. That was not even on the radar. I think I could've stayed at Southern and survived and done well at Southern."[131]

George held a vision of theological education that went beyond the categories of the progressive divinity school or denominational seminary. In other words, he wanted to be a part of a school that was committed to excellent academic and ecumenical scholarship more than a traditional denominational seminary. He also desired the school to be more orthodox and evangelical than a traditional divinity school in a university context.

George explains his reasoning for leaving the SBTS to start Beeson Divinity School at Samford University in Birmingham, Alabama: "It was really because a sense of God's call on my life to do this and the sense of the vision for the school that we needed this kind of place."[132] He believed that God was calling him to leave the SBTS to start "a place that was not captured by any one denomination, that was evangelical, rock solid conservative in its core, honored the Bible, believed the Bible, and yet could train students in a place where we could learn from one another. Be evangelical, interdenominational."[133] He admits, "Even though I'm a dyed-in-the-wool Southern Baptist, that's the kind of theologian I am. I'm an evangelical, even a kind of ecumenical theologian, so this was a good place to do that and I didn't find places like that just bursting out all over the place."[134]

George viewed Fuller Theological Seminary, Gordon-Conwell Theological Seminary, and Trinity Evangelical Divinity School as models of theological education: "The early days of Fuller, I would say that was a model. Gordon-Conwell, up near Boston is kind of a model. Trinity, near Chicago. There were schools like that that were doing something like this on a different scale in a different context, but in our region of the country

---

130. George, interview by Musgraves at Birmingham, AL, on August 18, 2014.
131. George, interview by Musgraves at Birmingham, AL, on August 18, 2014.
132. George, interview by Musgraves at Birmingham, AL, on August 18, 2014.
133. George, interview by Musgraves at Birmingham, AL, on August 18, 2014.
134. George, interview by Musgraves at Birmingham, AL, on August 18, 2014.

and in our kind of world, there was no such thing."[135] He believed God had called him to start an evangelical, interdenominational divinity school in Birmingham, Alabama.

Birmingham, Alabama (1988–present)

The Founding of Beeson Divinity School

At the request of Samford's President Tom Corts, Timothy George founded Beeson Divinity School, known for the first six months as "Samford Divinity School."[136] On February 9, 1988, Samford's Board of Trustees voted to begin a divinity school. The *Baptist Press* reported, "Samford to Start Divinity School."[137] Samford became the first "Southern Baptist affiliated university to offer the master of divinity."[138] The local need for theological education and ministry training in Alabama was great. Samford's Provost explained how "3,500 ministers without ministerial degrees now serve Alabama churches."[139]

George recounts, "On June 1 of that year, I arrived on campus to organize the work of Beeson Divinity School."[140] He began that work with prayers and with only modest means. He remembers, "I was given a broom closet of an office in Samford Hall. We had no facilities, no faculty, no curriculum, and only the promise of funding yet to come. I spent most of that first day in prayer asking the Lord to send us the students we would need to begin this new school in the fall."[141]

Denominational Opposition

Timothy George needed spiritual strength and resiliency as he faced adverse reactions from other leaders in theological education. He recalls, "I think I'd been here a week or two when all of the six SBC seminary presidents issued a common press release blasting President Corts and me for

---

135. George, interview by Musgraves at Birmingham, AL, on August 18, 2014.
136. Musgraves, "Founding Saints," 15.
137. Nunnelly and Knox, "Samford to Start Divinity School."
138. Nunnelly and Knox, "Samford to Start Divinity School," para. 5.
139. Nunnelly and Knox, "Samford to Start Divinity School," para. 9.
140. George, "Twenty Years of Gratitude," 1.
141. George, "Twenty Years of Gratitude," 1.

trying to start something that had never been done before."[142] The *Baptist Press* reported the press release from presidents from all six of the SBC denominational seminaries, saying, "Unfortunately, we think this action takes Southern Baptists not forward, but two steps backward."[143]

The divinity school's benefactor Ralph Waldo Beeson expected the school to be "Christian, Protestant, evangelical, and interdenominational."[144] While Mr. Beeson was not a trained theologian, he knew what he wanted the school to be, and he understood the importance of staying faithful to the historic Christian faith. George said, "In the early days of our school, he would call me and say, 'Now Timothy, I want you to keep things orthodox down there!' (Mr. Beeson lived on Shades Mountain and could look down on our campus from his home.)"[145] The Samford University Board of Trustees set as the confessional standard of the school "The Baptist Faith and Message" (1963).[146] Given the interdenominational or multi-confessional design of the divinity school, Mr. Beeson told President Corts: "You Baptists do a lot of good, but you can learn from others. And you ought to share with others what you already know."[147]

The *Baptist Press* reported that Mr. Beeson donated:

> $4.2 million as a beginning nucleus to start an interdenominational divinity school at Samford. Begun during the fall of 1988, the school was the first interdenominational divinity school in the nation on the campus of a Southern Baptist college or university. The Samford board of trustees subsequently voted to name the school in honor of Beeson and his late father.[148]

When Ralph Waldo Beeson died, he left a bequest to Samford to provide the following: "$17 million for endowment and support of Samford's Beeson School of Divinity; $8.5 million for scholarships in the school of divinity and Orlean Bullard Beeson School of Education at Samford, which is named for Beeson's late wife."[149]

---

142. George, interview by Musgraves at Birmingham, AL, on August 18, 2014.
143. Knox, "Seminary Presidents," para. 5.
144. George, "Twenty Years of Gratitude," 1.
145. George, "Twenty Years of Gratitude," 1.
146. Beeson Divinity School, "Confession of Faith," 3.
147. "Samford University Names Beeson," para. 5.
148. "Ralph W. Beeson," para. 9.
149. Nunnelley, "$38.8 Million Ralph Beeson Bequest," paras. 5–6.

George claims that "one needs only two things to build a great theological school."[150] The ingredients of greatness are not found in finances, facilities, or resources. He admits, "Those are wonderful assets to have, to be sure, and at Beeson we have been blessed with a healthy endowment, attractive facilities, and state of the art learning resources."[151] George, however, insists that "the two indispensable items are students who want to learn and teachers who love to teach."[152]

The Dean's Installation

Timothy George's leadership and vision for theological education began with his determination to uphold God's word and carry on faithful Christian doctrine to future generations. When George became the founding Dean of Beeson Divinity School at Samford University, on February 21, 1989, he proclaimed, "Let it be said for all posterity to hear that we stand without reservation for the total truthfulness of Holy Scripture and the great principles of historic Christian orthodoxy. On these essential values, we cannot, and we will not compromise."[153]

George's vision of theological education does not endorse an intellectualism devoid of genuine spiritual formation, growth in grace, and mission to the world. He says, "But we also know that godly teaching must be complemented by holy living, and so we commit ourselves to the disciplines of the Christian faith, to a life of prayer and worship, to witness and discipleship, and social compassion with justice and peace for every person made in the image of God."[154] He does not view these elements as being in competition or mutually exclusive to one another, but complementary and mutually-inclusive for the Christian minister.

The identity of the new school would not be, in George's words, "a haven for disaffected liberalism nor a bastion of raucous fundamentalism."[155] Instead, the school's identity, under George's leadership, would be

---

150. George, "Twenty Years of Gratitude," 2.
151. George, "Twenty Years of Gratitude," 2.
152. George, "Twenty Years of Gratitude," 2.
153. George, "Dean's Installation," 3.
154. George, "Dean's Installation," 3.
155. George, "Dean's Installation," 3.

"evangelical but also ecumenical, conservative but not irresponsible, confessional yet interdenominational."[156]

George's prayer at his installation service reveals his utmost desire for the new school and his highest priorities as the new dean:

> Above all, I pray that we might be a school where heart and head go hand in hand, where the love of God and pursuit of truth join forces in the formation of men and women, called by God, empowered by His Holy Spirit, equipped for the ministry of His church, sent forth into the world to bear witness to the grace of God revealed in the person of Jesus Christ, whom to know is life eternal.[157]

Carl F. H. Henry, who spoke at George's installation as dean, described the challenge that was before the new school: "The Christian movement needs clearly to exhibit the authority of Holy Scripture, the integration of intellect and piety in theological learning, and the high relevance of the Christian witness to secular society."[158] Henry called on George to take "seriously the missionary mandate of the church and to develop a program of theological formation and character building."[159]

Present Reflections

Thirty years after Timothy George came to Birmingham, Alabama, to start a divinity school, he reflects on the unique approach he has taken at Beeson regarding the faculty and theological curriculum. In an interview with Kevin Vanhoozer, he says, "Here at Beeson, we've had a little bit of a protest movement against the more recent way of fragmenting theology."[160] For example, when it comes to the faculty, "every professor here is a professor of divinity, not of this or that discipline within the body of divinity, but of divinity."[161] The designation of professor of divinity instead of only their field of study "theoretically means that they have the right to teach

---

156. George, "Dean's Installation," 3.

157. George, "Dean's Installation," 3.

158. See Henry, "Renewal of Theological Education," a seminary chapel sermon given at the Beeson Divinity School of Samford University in Birmingham, AL, on February 21, 1989; quoted in George, "What Were We Thinking?," 2–3.

159. Henry, "Renewal of Theological Education"; quoted in George, "What Were We Thinking?," 2–3.

160. George, "Conversation on Theology," 19:39–47.

161. George, "Conversation on Theology," 19:50–57.

and speak on any part of theology without claiming, 'That's not my area it's yours, or hers, or his.'"[162]

George revised the theological curriculum based on his perspective of historical theology and the needs of the evangelical and interdenominational context of Beeson Divinity School. He explains, "The other thing is what we've done with systematic theology and church history, we've abolished them."[163] He clarifies, "That is to say, we no longer have two stack poles and try to relate them disjunctively, but we brought them together in a sequence we call history and doctrine."[164] He describes the sequence of history and doctrine saying, "The effort is to look chronologically, but in a more systematic doctrinal way at the movement in the history of God's people of how these ideas have arisen and how they shape Christian life."[165] George's approach to Christian theology, built on his interpretation of Williams, Steinmetz, and Pelikan, has become known as "history and doctrine."[166] George's perspective on historical theology is the missing piece to the puzzle of how to train and teach students in the evangelical and interdenominational context of Beeson Divinity School.

Conclusion

Despite the difficult circumstances of Timothy George's early years in poverty-stricken Hell's Half-Acre in Chattanooga, Tennessee (1950–72), he discovered a love for reading, history, and public speaking through his local library and teachers. He became a Christian and received a call to ministry through his careful study of the Bible and the witness of a small Baptist church. He learned to be a theologian through debates with his Uncle Willie and the Mormon missionaries. He began traveling and preaching as a youth evangelist. He completed his undergraduate studies in history. While still a student and a young preacher, he married Denise.

---

162. George, "Conversation on Theology," 19:57–20:08.
163. George, "Conversation on Theology," 20:08–13.
164. George, "Conversation on Theology," 20:13–23.
165. George, "Conversation on Theology," 20:23–35.
166. See "Historical and Doctrinal Studies," Beeson Divinity School. "Unique in theological education, Beeson teaches theology and church history together in an integrated four-course sequence. Students learn key doctrines such as Scripture, Christology, Pneumatology, justification, creation, and anthropology as they unfold and develop in the history of the Christian church."

George completed his theological education and ministry training, graduate and doctoral studies, at Harvard Divinity School in Cambridge, Massachusetts (1972–79). During this time, he began a lifetime of learning from three key figures: George Huntston Williams, David Steinmetz, and Jaroslav Pelikan.

George started teaching historical theology in Louisville, Kentucky (1978–88). His calling to *keep truth alive* developed and matured through his classroom teaching and writings. He became known as an intellectual leader in the Southern Baptist denomination whose theological commitments were evangelical and conservative.

The apex of George's journey was his founding of Beeson Divinity School of Samford University in Birmingham, Alabama (1988–2019). George became an administrator in theological education, pioneering a model of theological education on a Baptist university campus that was both evangelical and interdenominational. At Beeson, he made a unique contribution to the theological curriculum by establishing a "history and doctrine" sequence instead of systematic theology and church history. As of July 1, 2019, George retired and "transitioned from dean to research professor, teaching church history and doctrine."[167] On May 5, 2020, the Samford University Board of Trustees named him the Distinguished Professor of Divinity.[168]

Chapter 2 has provided the biographical context of Timothy George's early life to his founding of Beeson Divinity School. In light of this biographical context, the best way to understand George's perspective on historical theology and its conceptual formation is to better understand George Huntston Williams (chapter 3), David Steinmetz (chapter 4), and Jaroslav Pelikan (chapter 5) by examining their biographical and professional contexts, historical and theological approaches, and key thoughts and contributions.

---

167. "Timothy George," para. 1.
168. "Timothy George," para. 2.

3

A Holy Calling, to Keep Truth Alive
George Huntston Williams (1914–2000)

> Theology that is truly biblical and evangelical is done for, with, and in the context of this enlarged Ecclesia for which Christ died.
>
> —TIMOTHY GEORGE

Introduction

THIS CHAPTER FOCUSES ON the influence of George Huntston Williams on Timothy George's understanding of historical theology and Christian doctrine. It offers a brief profile of Williams and identifies his major contributions that influenced George's approach to historical theology in terms of his calling and work.

Significant people and events from Williams's early life, education, and career provide the context to his historical and theological approach in the areas of church history as a theological discipline, ecumenism, and social activism. This chapter will then demonstrate the ways in which Timothy George received, recognized, and realized the legacy of George Huntston Williams in his work as a historical theologian.

This chapter is an integral part of this book by describing and analyzing George Huntston Williams as one of the three key figures that shaped Timothy George's understanding of historical theology in the areas of history and doctrine, Evangelicals and Catholics Together (ECT) and

The Manhattan Declaration. The central question of this book, Timothy George's understanding of historical theology, has been established in terms of significance (chapter 1) and biographical context (chapter 2). Now this chapter introduces the first of three key influencers, George Huntston Williams, who will be shown to shape Timothy George's understanding of historical theology (chapters 3–5).

Education and Career (1914–2000)

Early Life

George Huntston Williams was born "George Pease Williams" in Huntsburg, Ohio, to David Rhys Williams and Lucy Adams Williams on April 7, 1914, which was the same year that his father graduated from Harvard Divinity School. According to Timothy George, Williams changed his name to George Huntston Williams "to ward off insensitive school-yard taunts as a young boy he constructed a more elegant middle name for himself, and this is how he was known for the rest of his life: George Huntston Williams."[1]

Williams recalled how his mother's "loving understanding of all individuals in their diversity encouraged me in the study of their varied tongues."[2] He also recognized his father's influence in his life in terms of ministerial activity and social concerns. He wrote about his father's preaching and how his "prophetic sermons opened for me the vision of that world where thrones are crumbled and where kings are dust."[3] Williams's

---

1. George, "Holy Calling," para. 1. See Adams, "George Huntston Williams," 6. Adams noted, "Williams later on adopted the middle name Huntston, invented intentionally to resemble the word Huntsburg, since he had often been teased by his peers for his baptismal name, Pease. His grandparents Pease were never willing to accept the substitution and continued to call him George Pease Williams."

2. Williams, *Radical Reformation*. Quoted in Adams, "George Huntston Williams," 7.

3. Adams, "George Huntston Williams," 7; see also p. 5. During Williams's father's graduation ceremony at Harvard Divinity School, his father "arose and approached the podium. The faculty member in charge gestured for him to return to his seat, but instead of acquiescing he beckoned for the faculty member to take his seat. It is said that President Eliot gave a welcoming gesture." What came next became the theme of his father's ministry and would characterize Williams's leadership as a theological educator. His father spoke to the Harvard graduation ceremony with "the eloquence for which he was later to become noted, Williams asserted that theological education at Harvard fell short if it did not show concern for social justice." George Huntston Williams later became a

paternal grandparents contributed to his understanding of social action. Through family stories, Williams received the value of "social action as a means of effecting social change."[4]

Education

George Williams studied at St. Lawrence University in Canton, New York. William L. Fox, the President of St. Lawrence University (2009–present), was a former student of Williams at Harvard Divinity School and later developed a friendship with him. He recalled how Williams "revealed one day a detail of his early life that has stayed with me ever since as a significant parable. George Huntston Williams was only a C student at St. Lawrence."[5]

Williams studied at Meadville Theological School of the University of Chicago. He has been described by Timothy George as a "Unitarian who did not deny the Holy Trinity."[6] Williams explained why when he said, "My professor at the University of Chicago, Wilhelm Pauck, egged me on in a way without his knowing it, in my effort to grasp the history of the dogma of the Trinity formulation at the Council of Nicea in 325."[7] Pauck told Williams, "'As a born Unitarian, Mr. Williams, you can never understand the doctrine of the Trinity.' So that was a factor by way of determined reaction in my life. I resolved to show him I can."[8]

---

significant theological educator, emphasizing social justice at the same school where his father gave that charge.

4. Adams, "George Huntston Williams," 7. The paternal grandfather, David Thomas Williams, served as a pastor in a rural town that was caught up in a bitter labor-management dispute between coal miners and the owners. In the middle of a harsh winter, the owners prevented the miners from using their homes or accessing credit from local stores. In support of the miners, David Williams invited them to come stay inside his local church building and then raised funds for their care. Adams, "George Huntston Williams," 8.

5. Fox, "Honoring the C Student," para. 8.

6. George, "Holy Calling," para. 4.

7. Williams interviewed by John A. Buehrens, "George H. Williams: The Last Interview," a subsection of the "Williams, George Huntston" entry from the Harvard Square Library.

8. Williams interviewed by Buehrens. Williams, when speaking of his belief in the Trinity, would "refer to the Divine Triad" (George, "Remembering George Huntston Williams," 5:52–54). Smith claims that Williams did this for two reasons. First, Williams wanted to "express the core conviction of historic Christian faith, the Father, the Son, the Holy Spirit" (5:58–6:05). Second, according to Smith, Williams did not want to "wave a

In 1939 Williams completed his Bachelor of Divinity dissertation on "Tillich's Doctrine of Sin." James Adams estimated that this work was likely the first dissertation on Tillich in English.[9] Williams went on to complete his doctoral dissertation in 1946, and it was published in 1951 as *The Norman Anonymous of 1100 A.D.*[10]

Harvard Divinity School

George Huntston Williams began his teaching career at Harvard in 1947. At that time, the dean of Harvard Divinity School, Willard Sperry, did not offer Williams an enthusiastic welcome. In their first conversation he said, "I'm afraid, Mr. Williams, that there is not much of a future here for you."[11] Ann Braude comments about the status of the school during this time period: "In the 1940s HDS had been a near moribund institution."[12] When Dean Sperry welcomed Williams he was not optimistic about the future of the school. Williams, however, became instrumental in ensuring the future of Harvard Divinity School, and his career there lasted thirty-four years.

Williams reflected on his time serving as acting dean of the Divinity School in the 1950s: "That's an important aspect of my career, having been singled out by beloved Dean Willard Sperry to do what could be done at a time when it was not certain whether we'd have a Harvard Divinity School much longer, so precarious was its grip on institutional life; with the possible prospect of its being relocated in conjunction with Meadville Theological School in Chicago."[13] Adams noted the ecumenical aim of Williams's brief

---

red flag in front of people that might find offense at the language but might still leave the door open for a conversation" (6:06–15).

9. Adams, "George Huntston Williams," 2.

10. Williams, *Norman Anonymous of 1100 A.D.* Before Williams completed his dissertation, he started teaching church history at the Starr King School for the Ministry, which was a Unitarian school in Berkeley, and also at the Pacific School of Religion, which was a Congregational school. He began his doctoral studies at the University of California and then transferred to Union Theological Seminary in New York. See Hutchison et al., "Memorial Minute for George H. Williams."

11. Hutchison et al., "Memorial Minute for George H. Williams," para. 5.

12. Braude, "Short Half-Century," 369–80.

13. Williams, interviewed by Buehrens.

work as dean.[14] During this time, Williams taught courses[15] and wrote his major work titled *The Radical Reformation*, which was published in 1962.[16] Students benefited from Williams's ability to recall and recount not only the details of a period or figure in church history, but also the emotional tone and significance of that historical moment. He was able to create meaningful, teachable moments throughout his church history courses.

Major Contributions from George Huntston Williams

Church History as a Theological Discipline

In describing Williams's approach to the vocation of a church historian, James Luther Adams wrote, "The church historian accordingly writes of the past not merely for the past itself, but also for its impact on the present."[17] Adams recounts how John T. McNeill instructed Williams that "as church historian he should speak from his own community of faith, ever aware of its needs."[18] Adams wrote about Williams, "The past has never been for him a sanctuary in which to hide from the present. For one thing, it is capable of ringing the alarm, recalling the present church to its authentic mission."[19]

Williams's accomplishments were summarized by Franklin H. Little of Temple University when he said, "He is a credible witness, as both scholar and churchman. He has taken his stand with a 'new Church History,' well beyond most earlier writers—to whom Christian history was either an exercise in filial devotion or an attempt to present the history of Christianity

---

14. Adams, "George Huntston Williams," 11. Adams said of Williams: "Later, as Acting Dean of Harvard Divinity School he aimed to introduce an ecumenical pattern which previously had been neglected."

15. See George, "Remembering George Huntston Williams," 3:32–54. George Williams's brilliance as a teacher and his mastery of church history inspired students. A former student recounted, "I was absolutely amazed going into the classroom because George Williams knew everything. He just knew everything, encyclopedic and sensitive to all these different movements of God's work in and through the church, not perfectly realized by his people, but still just having the touch of God."

16. Williams, *Radical Reformation*.

17. Adams, "George Huntston Williams," 3.

18. Adams, "George Huntston Williams," 6.

19. Adams, "George Huntston Williams," 6.

as a sterile sector of the history of mankind."[20] In other words, Williams did not reduce his historical work to simplistic devotion or detached observations.

Robert M. Kingdon of the University of Wisconsin, Madison, said of Williams, "One of George Huntston Williams's most important contributions to scholarship has surely been in the history of ecclesiology."[21] Kingdon explained Williams's achievement when he said, "The distinction, which he first drew more than twenty years ago in his monumental studies of the Radical Reformation, between a 'Magisterial Reformation' of Lutherans, Zwinglians, Calvinists, and Anglicans on one hand, and a 'Radical Reformation' of Anabaptists, Spiritualists, and Evangelical Rationalists on the other, has influenced an entire generation of specialists in the period."[22]

Williams taught church history during a time when the purpose and significance of the discipline was called into question. For example, in December 1950, James Hasting Nichols addressed the American Society of Church History.[23] Nichols said, "One might venture the opinion that the teaching of church history has less effect on the attitude and thinking of theological students than has any other major disciplines, such as biblical studies, theology, ethics, perhaps even religious education."[24] Nichols posed the question, "Is Church History holding its own as a department of theology?"[25] Thus, he offered a more direct question to evaluate the significance of church history when he asked, "Does it convey religious insight in significant patterns of interpretation?"[26]

Williams argued for the value and function of church history as a theological discipline rather than church history as merely secular scientific historiography.[27] The secular scientific historiographical approach can

---

20. Littell, "Periodization of History," 18.

21. Kingdon, "Peter Martyr Vermigli," 198.

22. Kingdon, "Peter Martyr Vermigli," 198. See Williams, "Introduction," 19–38; Williams, "Studies in the Radical Reformation," 46; Williams, *Radical Reformation*, xxiii–xxxi.

23. Nichols, "Art of Church History," 3–9.

24. Nichols, "Art of Church History," 3–9.

25. Nichols, "Art of Church History," 3–9.

26. Nichols, "Art of Church History," 3–9.

27. See George, "George Huntston Williams," 17. George identifies Williams's historiography of church history in Williams's following essays: "Church History," 145–78; "Century of Church History at Harvard," 85–102; Smith and Williams, "In Defense of Church History."

be traced back to the fifteenth century with the father of modern humanistic historiography, Leonardo Bruni. Bruni wrote, "For, after all, history is an easy subject; there is nothing in its study subtle or complex. It consists in the narration of the simplest matters of fact which, once grasped, are readily retained in the memory."[28] In the nineteenth century, Leopold von Ranke claimed that the purpose of the historian was to reconstruct the past *"wie es eigentlich gewesen"* (as it really happened).[29] Williams did not claim that the task of church history was less than the scientific historiographical approach; it actually included so much more.

George Williams in his chapter "Church History" in Arnold Nash's book *Protestant Thought in the Twentieth Century: Whence and Whither?* supported the "possibility that a very important supplementary understanding of Church history is vouchsafed to those standing committedly within the historic community of faith."[30] This approach, however, was in competition with another approach known as secular, a reductionist form described as scientific church history articulated by Ephraim Emerton (1851–1935), professor of ecclesiastical history at Harvard Divinity School from 1882–1918.

Williams noted that on several occasions Emerton argued[31] "that all theological presuppositions must be strenuously eliminated from the study of Church history and rejoiced that for the most part Church historians had indeed acquiesced in the fusion of ecclesiastical and secular history, the former being but a chapter of the whole."[32] Williams pointed out that the opposition to the *scientific* approach by Emerton was the *subjective* approach by Arthur Cushman McGiffert.

Williams also described a mediatory group best represented by the work of a Southern Baptist, Albert Henry Newman. Williams draws the reader's attention to the introduction to Newman's work, *A Manual of Church History*,[33] which gave six reasons for studying church history, notably "pointing out not only that it is a vast commentary on Scripture which shows us how the slightest departure from New Testament principles has resulted in error—here the sectarian concern is operative—but also that the

---

28. Quoted in Harbison, *Christianity and History*, 31.
29. Von Ranke, *Theory and Practice of History*, xix–xx.
30. Williams, "Church History," 148.
31. Emerton, "Study of Church History," 1; "Definition of Church History," 53–68.
32. Williams, "Church History," 150.
33. Newman, *Manual of Church History*.

study of Church history nevertheless increases charity and mutual understanding, thus promoting Church unity—here the newer interdenominational inserts is to the fore."[34] By using the phrase "to the fore,"[35] Williams meant that the interdenominational activity of this time period heightens, or brings to the surface, the relevance of the study of church history and its ability to promote special care and consideration between church leaders and scholars of different Christian denominations.

Williams recognized Methodist John Fletcher Hurst of Drew Theological Seminary (1834–1903) as the representative of the new historiography of the twentieth century, "situated within the denominational context but keenly conscious of the universal Church and thoroughly committed to, and informed by, the newer German methodology."[36] Another representative of the mediatory school was George Park Fisher (1837–1909), professor of ecclesiastical history at Yale. Williams regards Fisher's work, *History of the Christian Church* (1887), as "denominational-based theological and apologetic interest in the subject."[37]

Williams commented about Fisher's successor at Yale, Williston Walker (1860–1922). He viewed Walker's writing as a stark contrast to Fisher's approach. Williams wrote about Walker's work: "Yet one detects in his works and particularly in his *History of the Christian Church* (1918) the absence of any sense of his writing from the interior of the Church."[38]

In Defense of Church History

Williams gave a clear definition and clarification of his historiography at Trinity Evangelical Divinity School in a lecture titled, "In Defense of Church History: A Minister with Historical Perspective."[39] He began by acknowledging his previous pastoral ministry and expressing that he still views himself as a minister. He said, "I was a minister nearby at the Church of the Christian Union in Rockford, Illinois. I came to Rockford, my only actual parish (regarding myself still, however, very much a minister)."[40]

34. Williams, "Church History," 151–52.
35. Williams, "Church History," 151–52.
36. Williams, "Church History," 152.
37. Williams, "Church History," 153.
38. Williams, "Church History," 154.
39. Smith and Williams, "In Defense of Church History," 400.
40. Smith and Williams, "In Defense of Church History," 400.

He clarified the purpose of his lecture by first saying what church history is *not*. He said, "My topic is the 'Defense of Church History'- a strange topic. Now Church history is clearly not the same as missionary history, nor is it identical with ecclesiastical history- a point fundamental to my presentation."[41] Again he clarified, "but missionary history is not the same as Church history."[42]

Williams distinguished *ecclesiastical* history from *church* history. He said, "Ecclesiastical history, as I am using it, is the use by historians or archivists of the material gathered by a community, being preserved records from the convent, from the monasteries, from episcopal palaces, from the theologians and the universities created by Christendom."[43] The problem with *ecclesiastical* history, as Williams understood it, was that "ecclesiastical history is annexed to general history. I also recognize that ecclesiastical history can fructify other disciplines like sociology, demography, even psychology."[44]

Williams argued what church history is *not* and then explained what it *is*. He said, "What needs defense, however, is not ecclesiastical history but Church history, that is to say, the history of the community of faith in time and space."[45] Williams also clarified, "I am not defending the tendentious or polemical history."[46]

Williams began, "My first point is that Church history is comprehensive. To be entitled to full status as a branch of divinity, it is in this regard the discipline in the divinity school or seminary that is concerned with the one, holy, catholic Church."[47] First, Williams addressed the role of the church historian as the one responsible for recounting and reinterpreting church history. He said, "Therefore, we are the scribes and interpreters of this large body of material."[48]

Second, Williams defined the comprehensive scope of the church in two main categories of space and time: "Its comprehensiveness is itself a part of our responsibility: keeping it comprehensive, not only in space,

---

41. Smith and Williams, "In Defense of Church History," 401.
42. Smith and Williams, "In Defense of Church History," 401.
43. Smith and Williams, "In Defense of Church History," 400.
44. Smith and Williams, "In Defense of Church History," 401.
45. Smith and Williams, "In Defense of Church History," 401.
46. Smith and Williams, "In Defense of Church History," 402.
47. Smith and Williams, "In Defense of Church History," 403.
48. Smith and Williams, "In Defense of Church History," 403.

which is fairly easy for us to do (in a missionary-minded school like this one, in a global society like ours today, concerned with Latin America, Asia, we don't have to be reminded not to be parochial), but also, involving an ecumenicity in time."[49]

Third, Williams argued for the necessity of a comprehensive general stewardship regardless of specialization. He said, "I feel that the Church historian, regardless of the degree to which he specializes (and he must specialize like any other craftsman in other disciplines), must do this."[50]

Williams distinguished the type of work that the church historian does from the work of the ecclesiastical historian. He said, "The Church historian, I think, is distinguished from the ecclesiastical historian in that the Church historian does take this larger thing into consideration."[51] He explained, "Church history in this large sense, seeing it even despite our specialization within it and our carefully worked out footnotes, finds the Church historian in charge of, not a relativizing discipline, but a harmonizing or irenic discipline, which sees a large field."[52]

Williams used the idea of love and its meaning as an example of the large field. He said, "The meaning of love is itself evolved, and it's extremely interesting to see in various contexts. Therefore the Church historian, by having a sense of the whole, although he specializes in a part, will not be caught in some misunderstanding of the great concepts of the one, holy, Catholic church, whatever his or her confession may be."[53]

Williams raised another point when he said, "The second defense of Church history is that it is the discipline in divinity that is concerned with the credo in the communion of saints."[54] By "credo" he means the Christian faith or Christian beliefs. By "communion of saints" he is arguing that the church history worth defending is the study of not only names, dates, and details, but the faith and credo of Christians throughout time and space.

Williams wrote, "My third conception in defense of Church history is that it is an ally of theology and Christian ethics, of missiology and the comparative study of religion, in upholding true Christian liberty."[55] He argued

---

49. Smith and Williams, "In Defense of Church History," 403.
50. Smith and Williams, "In Defense of Church History," 403.
51. Smith and Williams, "In Defense of Church History," 404.
52. Smith and Williams, "In Defense of Church History," 404.
53. Smith and Williams, "In Defense of Church History," 404.
54. Smith and Williams, "In Defense of Church History," 404.
55. Smith and Williams, "In Defense of Church History," 406.

that this discipline is not inferior to or in competition to other branches of study. On the contrary, church history according to Williams complements and supports all the other disciplines in the theological curriculum.

Ecumenism

Williams has been recognized as the leading pioneer of "ecumenical scholarship in the service of Protestant-Catholic relationships."[56] James Adams noted that Williams "served from 1962 to 1965 as an official Observer at Vatican Council II."[57] It was during this time, Timothy George explains, that the highlight of Williams's ecumenical activity began when "Williams had first met the Polish bishop at Vatican II and developed a strong friendship with him during a sabbatical year in Krakow."[58] The strong bond between Williams and Wojtyła motivated Williams to write the first major intellectual biography of the pope, *The Mind of John Paul II*.[59] He became the first "Protestant theologian to be admitted by the new pope into the Order of Saint Gregory the Great."[60]

Williams commented on the circumstances surrounding his reception into the "Knighthood of St. Gregory the Great from Pope Paul II."[61] He said that his knighthood was "pressed forward by ecumenically inspired Greater Boston Catholics" because they recognized Williams's ecumenical emphasis and wanted to express gratitude for his expertise with Pope John Paul II's writings. For example, at that time, Williams said that he "had read everything that John Paul had written, including his plays."[62]

Williams was one of the first religious commentators to publicly identify Karol Józef Wojtyła as the likely candidate to be the next pope.[63] He discovered Wojtyła during the second Vatican Council in Rome where

---

56. Hehier, "Professor George Huntston Williams," 347.
57. Adams, "George Huntston Williams," 3.
58. George, "John Paul II," 267–70.
59. Williams, *Mind of John Paul II*.
60. George, "John Paul II," 267–70.
61. Williams, interviewed by Buehrens.
62. Williams, interviewed by Buehrens.
63. See "Williams, George Huntston (1914–2000)." Forrest Church noted, "Williams had the unique distinction of having been the only person in the United States to predict the election of Pope John Paul II."

Willams was attending "St. Peter's Vatican as Observer, at all four sessions."[64] The Second Vatican Council issued an important document titled *Decree on Ecumenism*.[65] J. Bryan Hehier claimed that "George H. Williams exemplified the characteristics needed to show the way for ecumenism."[66]

Williams's early writing focused on the ideas of Frederic Henry Hedge (1805–90), who placed a special emphasis on ecumenism.[67] He was interested in Hedge's ideas primarily because he was as an ecumenist. He wrote early in his career about the ecumenism of Hedge in *Rethinking the Unitarian Relationship with Protestantism: An Examination of the Thought of Henry Hedge*.[68]

Williams reflected, "I felt I was legitimized here at Harvard in my effort to be a church historian for all denominations: Protestant, Catholic, Greek Orthodox, and the rest that came in, as well as the various kinds of Protestants, by reason of the pioneer work of Hedge."[69] For Williams, Hedge's work was foundational to his own ecumenical priorities. Williams said, "Hedge was the first in America to use the term 'ecumenical' in its modern interfaith connotation."[70]

Social Activism

George H. Williams studied under James Luther Adams, "his first teacher in theology and ethics who reinforced an already keen sense of social responsibility."[71] Williams also recognized his father's contribution to his sense of social activism. He recalled, "My life was influenced by my father's prophetic stand on a number of issues. And that went back in his own family, not only through the male line, but in that of his mother and his grandmother during the strikes in Scranton, Pennsylvania."[72] Williams

---

64. Williams, interviewed by Buehrens.
65. Abbott, *Documents of Vatican II*, 341–66.
66. Hehier, "Professor George Huntston Williams," 349.
67. See Adams, "George Huntston Williams," 13. Adams noted, "Hedge served as the first professor of ecclesiastical history (1857–1876) at Harvard Divinity School. In this position he was, then, one of Williams's predecessors."
68. Williams, *Rethinking the Unitarian Relationship*.
69. Williams, interviewed by Buehrens.
70. Williams, interviewed by Buehrens.
71. George, "Historian for All Seasons," 16–17.
72. Williams, interviewed by Buehrens.

described his father as a "spirited feminist"[73] because it was his father who gave the "oration when Susan B. Anthony, a Quaker, once a member of his Rochester congregation, was received into the Hall of Fame."[74]

Timothy George observed the activism of Williams in three main areas that characterized the major cultural issues in America from the 1950s to the 1970s. The first period is the 1950s, during the McCarthy era. In this period Williams argued for the "principle of 'conscientious reticence.'"[75] In opposition to the methods of U.S. Senator Joseph McCarthy, Williams made the case against involuntary informants in the article, "Reluctance to Inform."[76] George explains that Williams "defended the right of the sensitized conscience against forced informing."[77]

The second period of Williams's activism is the 1960s, during the Civil Rights era and Vietnam War. He demonstrated his firm support of racial equality by marching "in Montgomery with Martin Luther King, Jr., a former auditor in his courses in church history."[78] Williams energetically participated in ecumenical activities that protested "the racism which he had opposed in determining to attend the inner-city East High School in Rochester and, later, in marching in Montgomery.... Asa Davis, one of his doctoral students, unbeknownst to Williams, brought the young Martin Luther King to one of his lectures at Harvard. In the lecture he predicted that the next great theologian would be black."[79]

Williams made a strong protest against the war in Vietnam. Timothy George points out that along with "Richard John Neuhaus, he opposed the war in Vietnam."[80] The setting for Williams's impromptu protest was the Arlington Street Church in Boston, Massachusetts. He performed what has been described as "the ultimate symbolic act of protest."[81] His action of protest was that he "began to burn draft cards—in this case in the pulpit."[82] The

---

73. Williams, interviewed by Buehrens.

74. Williams, interviewed by Buehrens. Williams remembered when in Susan B. Anthony's honor, it was "her pew that my father saw to being appropriately marked."

75. George, "Holy Calling," para. 8.

76. Williams, "Reluctance to Inform," 229–55.

77. George, "Holy Calling," para. 8.

78. George, "Holy Calling," para. 8.

79. Adams, "George Huntston Williams," 12.

80. Adams, "George Huntston Williams," 12.

81. Hutchison et al., "Memorial Minute for George H. Williams," para. 16.

82. Hutchison et al., "Memorial Minute for George H. Williams," para. 16.

immediate reaction to Williams, the esteemed Harvard professor, making this type of stand in this setting against the Vietnam War was utter shock and surprise. For example, his act of protest "apparently left the principal speaker, William Sloan Coffin, at an uncharacteristic loss for words."[83]

The third period of Williams's activism is the 1970s, when even before the landmark case of *Roe v. Wade*, Williams wrote and spoke against the practice of abortion on demand.[84] At one time, he held the position of president of the National Right to Life Committee. Williams gave a sermon defending the unborn at Harvard's Memorial Church. It was after his sermon that he "received a blow to the head from a critic in the congregation who was enraged by his pro-life perspective."[85] In 1973 Williams addressed the national group, Americans United For Life, to urge young people to be involved in the pro-life movement. He said, "In these crucial hours for mankind, let each of us be unafraid and unfailing in this noble and historic effort to restore in this land the right to continuing life of every human life, born and unborn."[86]

Reception and Transmission by Timothy George

Timothy George describes his initial impression of George Huntston Williams when he started as a student at Harvard Divinity School. He writes, "When I arrived at Harvard University in 1972, he was already a legend in that place and widely known elsewhere as one of the leading church historians of his time."[87] He cherished the time when he served as a teaching fellow for Williams. He assisted him "for a couple of those years when we were meeting at Sever Hall."[88]

George wrote about the personal impact Williams had made on him. He recalled Williams's participation at the morning prayer service held in Appleton Chapel. He described the frequency of Williams's attendance in

---

83. Hutchison et al., "Memorial Minute for George H. Williams," para. 16.

84. Williams, "Religious Residues and Presuppositions," 10–75.

85. George, "Holy Calling," para. 8.

86. Williams, message to National Youth Pro-Life Coalition Convention. Quoted in Broek, "Rallying the Right-to-Lifers," 101.

87. George, "Holy Calling," para. 1.

88. George, "Remembering George Huntston Williams," 4:24–32.

Retrieval for the Sake of Renewal

terms of "always"[89] going and saying that "without fail, he would be there."[90] While the speakers and topics addressed in the 1970s in a morning prayer service at Harvard consisted of a wide variety and addressed a wide range of concerns, he did not attend for those shifting topics. Williams attended, according to George, because of the continuity of three activities in every session of morning prayer: (1) "the Lord's prayer was said,"[91] (2) "a reading of the Scriptures,"[92] (3) and "the singing of a hymn."[93]

As a young divinity student, George accompanied Williams to morning prayer, and then he would walk to class with him. He asked Williams why he went to prayer every morning.[94] He replied, "This is so important that you begin your day in a time of prayer and reflection. It's going to shape the rest of your day."[95] George admired the devotional and reflective disciplines that Williams embodied. He commented on Williams's habit and approach to morning prayer, saying, "And that's the way his life was lived."[96]

George recognized the influence of Williams on his personal approach to ecumenism. He states this in a conversation with Jim Smith, another student who learned from Williams. He remarked, "Well, while we're still talking about ecumenism, it was George [Huntston Williams] who really taught me the importance of what I've come to call ecumenism of conviction not of accommodation."[97]

George appreciated Williams's ability to value the breadth of Christian movements but also maintains that he "also had depth, and he never wanted people to sort of play loose and fast with their hard-fought, hard-won convictions."[98] He learned from Williams that the pathway to unity with other Christians was not through compromise but through conviction. He recalled that it was Williams's position that "a person who had really deep convictions and was willing to defend them and talk about them was much closer to the heart of Christian unity than someone who simply sought

---

89. George, "Remembering George Huntston Williams," 4:32–37.
90. George, "Remembering George Huntston Williams," 4:40–46.
91. George, "Remembering George Huntston Williams," 4:52–57.
92. George, "Remembering George Huntston Williams," 4:57–5:00.
93. George, "Remembering George Huntston Williams," 5:00–5:01.
94. George, "Remembering George Huntston Williams," 5:02–06.
95. George, "Remembering George Huntston Williams," 5:10–17.
96. George, "Remembering George Huntston Williams," 5:18–20.
97. George, "Remembering George Huntston Williams," 9:58–10:08.
98. George, "Remembering George Huntston Williams," 10:10–20.

the least common denominator, 'Let's just hold hands and be nice' kind of philosophy of ecumenism."[99]

George links Williams's view of ecumenism with Williams's historiography. He said, "So I appreciated that fact that he was a person of conviction. He had deep convictions about many things. We've talked about some of them, and he encouraged that in his students. And he once said that the two parts of the creed that the church historian is to make meaningful are *Una Sancta*, the one holy Catholic and Apostolic church; and *Communio Sanctorum*, the church as the communion of saints."[100]

George claims that a theologian for *the church* must be a theologian for *the whole church*. He said, "An ecclesial theologian must also be an ecumenical theologian—ecumenical in the sound, orthodox sense of that word."[101] He explains, "That means, a pastor theologian is concerned with the entire people of God through the ages and also with the *missio Dei* throughout the entire *oikoumenc* today, that is, the whole inhabited world (Luke 2:1)."[102]

George clarifies the relationship between the community of faith from which the theologian stands and the wider community of faith. He says, "Such pastors honor and cherish the discrete traditions from which they come, but they also know themselves to belong to the one, holy, catholic, and apostolic church, which is the Body of Christ extended throughout time as well as space."[103] Therefore, he argues, "Theology that is truly biblical and evangelical is done for, with, and in the context of this enlarged Ecclesia for which Christ died."[104]

History and Doctrine

Timothy George carries on Williams's approach of "Church History as a Theological Discipline" through his method termed "History and Doctrine," which integrates the historical context with the doctrinal content to understand its meaning and development. As a professor of divinity, he often began his course "The Theology of the Reformers" with a lecture

---

99. George, "Remembering George Huntston Williams," 10:21–35.
100. George, "Remembering George Huntston Williams," 10:35–11:02.
101. George, "Foreword," to *The Pastor Theologian*, 8.
102. George, "Foreword," to *The Pastor Theologian*, 8.
103. George, "Foreword," to *The Pastor Theologian*, 8.
104. George, "Foreword," to *The Pastor Theologian*, 8.

capturing his approach to history and doctrine titled "Church History as a Theological Discipline."[105]

From a curriculum and administrative angle, George claims that Williams's perspective was "shaped in part by the fact that between 1947 and 1954 he was largely responsible for teaching the entire gamut of Church history, which he developed as a four-semester sequence: Ancient, Medieval, Reformation, and Modern (including American)."[106] Just as Williams taught George a four-semester sequence of the Christian doctrine and history, under George's administrative leadership, Beeson Divinity School offered in its history and doctrine curriculum a four-semester sequence covering the full scope of history and doctrine: "Patristic History and Doctrine,"[107] "Medieval and Reformation History and Doctrine," "Reformation and Early Modern History and Doctrine," and "Later Modern History and Doctrine."[108]

Williams specialized in Reformation Studies, coining the term used in his well-known work, *Radical Reformation*, a landmark publication. George has established himself as a specialist in the Reformation era through his works, *Theology of the Reformers*,[109] *Reading Scripture with the Reformers*, and by serving as the General Editor of the *Reformation Commentary Series*. Williams was also a determined generalist, teaching and writing on the whole of the Christian Tradition. Likewise, George does not limit his writing, research, and teaching to the Reformation, but addresses the grand scope of church history.

Evangelicals and Catholics Together (ECT)

Timothy George continues Williams's work of ecumenism through his involvement in the Baptist World Alliance and especially through the initiative known as ECT, Evangelicals and Catholics Together. John Woodbridge

---

105. George, "Church History as a Theological Discipline."

106. George, "Historian for All Seasons," 16.

107. When Matthew Levering made the comment, "I think to some degree, you can't be a great theologian unless you recover Augustine." Timothy George replied, "I'm glad you said that. I agree with that." See George, "Vatican II and Christian Unity."

108. "Historical and Doctrinal Studies," 33.

109. Williams wrote in the preface to the 3rd edition of *Radical Reformation*, "I wish to acknowledge with gratitude the encouragement occasioned by the dedications of four books to me . . . one on four reformers, including Menno Simmons by Dean Timothy George of Birmingham (1987)."

of TEDS remarks, "George, a brilliant essayist, church historian, and theologian, has been one of the principal Evangelical participants in ECT. It is quite difficult to imagine the existence of the ECT enterprise without his significant irenic involvement."[110] George was influenced by Williams's "strong interest in the Catholic church."[111] George observed three ways that Williams was interested in the Catholic Church, also pointing out Williams's underlying theological rationale.

First, George points out that Williams was "one of the very few Protestant observers at all four sessions of the Second Vatican Council."[112] Second, he acknowledges how Williams "became acquainted with the person who became Pope John Paul II, Karol Cardinal Wojtyla, when he was at Vatican II."[113] Third, he mentions that Williams "wrote a book about him called *The Mind of John Paul II*."[114] He reflects on the theological reason for Williams's interest in the Catholic Church, saying, "And this was something that he conveyed to me, and I'm sure to you and to all of his students: the importance of the unity of the body of Christ despite the brokenness and dividedness that we live with in a broken world today."[115]

George is not a stranger to the Vatican. He met three popes: Pope John Paul II in 2004,[116] Pope Benedict XVI in 2012,[117] and Pope Francis in 2014.[118] George recounts, "I first heard of Karol Wojtyla when I was a graduate student at Harvard University studying with the great church historian George Huntston Williams."[119]

---

110. Woodbridge, "Timothy George and Evangelical and Catholics Together," 263.

111. George, "Remembering George Huntston Williams," 7:32–35.

112. George, "Remembering George Huntston Williams," 7:36–42.

113. George, "Remembering George Huntston Williams," 7:46–53.

114. George, "Remembering George Huntston Williams," 7:53–56.

115. George, "Remembering George Huntston Williams," 7:56–8:09.

116. George, "Pope John Paul II," 8:54–9:52. George discussed the legacy of Pope John Paul II with Dr. George Weigel. Weigel is an expert about the late pope.

117. George comments on Benedict XVI as "maybe the greatest theologian to have become pope since Leo in the early church. I mean he is a remarkable thinker.... In some ways he's the great Augustinian theologian of our age." See George, "Vatican II and Christian Unity"; see also George, "Promise of Benedict XVI."

118. See George, "Our Francis, Too," para. 5. George comments: "Since the Roe v. Wade Supreme Court decision of 1973, Catholics and evangelicals in the United States have worked side by side to advocate for the sanctity of life. The pro-life community will have a strong ally in the new pope."

119. George, "John Paul II," 267–70.

Retrieval for the Sake of Renewal

George wrote the following regarding the definition of Roman Catholics: "It is not very difficult to define Roman Catholicism. At least, it is rather easy to say what makes one a Roman Catholic. A Roman Catholic is a person affiliated with a church whose bishop is in communion with the Bishop of Rome. That is very straightforward and quite accurate."[120]

George begins to define evangelicalism by first acknowledging that "Bebbington's evangelical quadrilateral has gained credence as a helpful summary of the essence of the evangelical faith."[121] He, however, seeks to improve and build upon Bebbington's definition. He first offers a general definition: "I suggest a simpler and even briefer definition: evangelicalism is a renewal movement within historic Christian orthodoxy."[122]

George qualifies his definition of evangelicalism both theologically and historically. First, in a theological sense he says, "Its theology and piety have been enriched by many diverse tributaries, including Puritanism, pietism, and Pentecostalism."[123] Second, in a historical sense he claims that modern evangelicalism received "its sense of identity as a distinctive faith community, what we might call the evangelical tradition, has been shaped decisively by three major episodes: the Protestant Reformation, the evangelical Awakening, and the fundamentalist-modernist controversy."[124]

George faced critics of his ecumenical efforts, like Dave Hunt. Hunt expressed public outrage and disappointment regarding the formation of ECT. Hunt wrote, "I believe the document represents the most devastating blow against the gospel in at least 1,000 years."[125] George responded with an editorial in *Christianity Today* wherein he described this new initiative as "an ecumenism of the trenches."[126] He clarified the meaning and purpose of ECT:

> Here is an ecumenism of the trenches born out of a common moral struggle to proclaim and embody the Gospel of Jesus Christ in a culture of disarray. This is not merely a case of politics making

---

120. George, "Between the Pope and Billy Graham," 125.
121. George, "Between the Pope and Billy Graham," 126.
122. George, "Between the Pope and Billy Graham," 126.
123. George, "Between the Pope and Billy Graham," 126.
124. George, "Between the Pope and Billy Graham," 126. For more on George's understanding of evangelicalism, see George, "Spectrum of Evangelicalism." See George's conversation with Woodbridge in "Great Shapers of Evangelicalism."
125. Hunt, "Gospel Betrayed," para. 6.
126. George, "Catholics and Evangelicals in the Trenches," para. 4.

strange bedfellows. It is more like Abraham bargaining with God for the minimal number of righteous witnesses required to spare the city of Sodom. For too long, ecumenism has been left to left-leaning Catholics and mainline Protestants. For that reason alone evangelicals should applaud this effort and rejoice at its progress.[127]

For George the foundational biblical basis for his ecumenical efforts in the ECT are John 17:19 and 17:21. George comments, "Both Catholic and Evangelical participants recognized that the only unity worth having was unity in the truth. They determined to practice an ecumenism of conviction, not an ecumenism of accommodation."[128]

In 1994 J. I. Packer wrote an essay defending ECT and his continued involvement in it titled, "Why I Signed It." He said, "I am a Protestant who thanks God for the wisdom, backbone, maturity of mind, conscience, and above all love for my Lord Jesus Christ that I often see among Catholics, and who sometimes has the joy of hearing Catholics say they see comparable fruits in Protestants."[129]

Packer viewed the formal relationship and statements between Evangelical and Catholic theologians within ECT as merely reflecting what was already happening informally. He believed that the initiative was "fuel for a fire that is already alight. The grassroots coalition at which the document aims is already growing. It can be argued that, so far from running ahead of God, as some fear, ECT is playing catch up to the Holy Spirit."[130]

George argues that the Vatican II council "should not be understood simply as an event within the Catholic Church. It should be recognized, rather, as perhaps the greatest ecclesial event of the twentieth century, with profound significance for all Christians."[131] He discussed the importance of

---

127. George, "Catholics and Evangelicals in the Trenches," para. 5.

128. George, "Unity," 3. See George's address to the Vatican: "*Unitatis Redintegratio* after 50 Years," 69–76. George discussed the topic of ecumenism with Chad Raith II in "Ecumenism: A Personal Journey." George also discussed the ECT, the topic of ecumenism, and *First Things* magazine with R. R. Reno in "Sharp-Elbow Ecumenism." George has also addressed his views on the Baptist movement and ecumenism: George, "Baptists and Ecumenism," 89–92.

129. Packer, "Why I Signed It," para. 14.

130. Packer, "Why I Signed It," para. 23.

131. George, "Theological Introduction," xx.

Retrieval for the Sake of Renewal

Vatican II with Catholic Theologian Mathew Levering.[132] He also discussed Vatican II with Thomas G. Guarino.[133]

Pope John XXIII on October 11, 1962 said, "The deposit of faith is one thing, and the manner in which it is expressed is another."[134] This viewpoint was expressed in earlier times and more recently. The idea can be found by early proponents such as Vincent of Lerins, John Damascene, and Thomas Aquinas, and more recently by Karl Barth. For example, Vincent addresses the use of the terms *homoousios* and *Theotokos*.[135] He argued that while these terms or specific words are new, the meaning conveyed through them is not.

George argues for a "reevaluation of the relationship between Scripture and tradition"[136] and for Evangelical theologians to consider using "*suprema scriptura* as an apposite phrase, one that recognizes the unique value of Scripture while also acknowledging a place for ecclesial tradition."[137] In agreement, Baptist theologian James Leo Garrett concludes that "*Suprema Scriptura*, not a quite literal and restricted *Sola Scriptura*, provides the most representative and accurate Protestant answer to the question as to the ranking of channels of religious authority."[138]

Kevin Vanhoozer remarks, "If *sola scriptura* means 'the Bible alone apart from the church and tradition,' it has no future. But this is not what *sola scriptura* means. *Sola scriptura* is a protest not against tradition as such but against the presumption that church tradition (interpretation) and Scripture (text) necessarily coincide."[139]

Pope John Paul II's emphasis on truth as the key ingredient for ecumenical dialogue was the inspiration and motivation for both Catholics and Evangelicals in the ECT movement to find a basis for conversation and cooperation. The basis for Evangelicals and Catholics was the pursuit of truth. Pope John Paul II said:

---

132. George, "Vatican II and Christian Unity." George said to Matthew Levering, "Vatican II was an ecumenical council, as the Catholic Church understands it, that had a profound impact on the direction of Christian faith in the 20th century continuing to today."

133. George, "Vatican 2: Semper Reformanda."

134. John XXIII, "Gaudet Mater Ecclesia," 792.

135. Vincent of Lérins, "*Commonitorium*, no. 22," 131–56; See Guarino, "Tradition and Doctrinal Development," 34–72.

136. George, "Theological Introduction," xxv.

137. George, "Theological Introduction," xxv.

138. Garrett, *Systematic Theology*, 207.

139. Vanhoozer, "Scripture and Tradition," 167.

A Holy Calling, to Keep Truth Alive

> Love for the truth is the deepest dimension of any authentic quest for full communion between Christians . . . . The unity willed by God can be obtained only by the adherence of all to the content of revealed faith in its entirety in matters of faith; compromise is in contradiction with God, who is Truth. In the body of Christ, 'the Way, and the Truth, and the Life' (John 14:6), who could consider legitimate a reconciliation brought about at the expense of the truth?[140]

The Manhattan Declaration

The legacy of social activism that Timothy George received from George Huntston Williams is best expressed through George's work on *The Manhattan Declaration*. George joined Chuck Colson and became a part of the Prison Fellowship Board of Directors when Carl F. H. Henry retired and passed the responsibility of the chair of the Theology Committee to him. In June of 2009 George gave the devotional at a meeting of the Prison Fellowship Board and recognized the *Barmen Declaration* on its seventy-fifth anniversary. He focused the attention of those present on the first article of the document, which states, "Jesus Christ, as he has tested for us in the Holy Scripture, is the one word of God which we have to hear and which we have to trust and obey in life and in death."[141] He made the point that those "who were present at Barmen that day, such as Pastor Martin Niemöller, experienced great suffering and persecution at the hands of the Nazis in the years following."[142] George remembers that by the end of this meeting, Colson exclaimed, "The church needs a *Barmen Declaration* for today!"[143]

George remembers how for the first time, "Catholic, Protestant, and Orthodox leaders stood together side-by-side and declared our common commitment to what we believed to be three of the most pressing, and increasingly contested, moral issues of our time."[144] The first issue was the sanctity of life.[145] George clarifies the meaning and scope of the term as sanctity "for every single person including the elderly, the weak, and the

---

140. Wojtyla, "Ut Unum Sint," 54, 58.
141. "Theological Declaration of Barmen," 124.
142. George, *Life, Marriage, and Religious Liberty*, xii-xiv.
143. George, *Life, Marriage, and Religious Liberty*, xiv.
144. George, *Life, Marriage, and Religious Liberty*, xiv.
145. George, *Life, Marriage, and Religious Liberty*, xiv.

pre-born, each of whom is uniquely made in the image of God (imago Dei) and is inherently worthy of respect and protection."[146] He defends and supports the pro-life movement.[147]

The second moral issue was the "historic institution of marriage."[148] George understands this union as "between one man and one woman, not for the sake of traditionalism but for the flourishing of families and the nurturing of children, an institution which is the cornerstone of society across civilizations."[149]

The third moral issue was religious freedom.[150] George defends this freedom "not only for Christians, but for all persons everywhere, and for religious institutions as well as for individuals, for synagogues, mosques, temples, and churches, and the work they do on behalf of the common good in education and benevolence."[151]

There are two significant differences between the *Barmen Declaration* and *The Manhattan Declaration*. The first difference is one of historical circumstance. George said, "We did not make the claim in 2009, nor should we make it today, that our present historical moment is analogous to the repression Jews, Christians, and many others experienced in Hitler's Germany."[152]

The second difference between the *Barmen Declaration* and *The Manhattan Declaration* is one of theological collaboration. George said, "The *Barmen Declaration* was written and signed by only Protestant (Lutheran and Reformed) Christians, whereas *The Manhattan Declaration* intentionally included Roman Catholic, Evangelical Protestant, and Eastern Orthodox voices."[153] He described this theological collaboration to be one of theological integrity and ecumenical cooperation without compromising

---

146. George, *Life, Marriage, and Religious Liberty*, xiv.

147. See George, "Defending Life"; George, "In the Shadow of the Clinic"; George, "Unplanned."

148. George, *Life, Marriage, and Religious Liberty*, xiv. See also George, "Marriage," Beeson Podcast; George, "Why Marriage Matters," Beeson Podcast.

149. George, *Life, Marriage, and Religious Liberty*, xiv.

150. George, *Life, Marriage, and Religious Liberty*, xiv.

151. George, *Life, Marriage, and Religious Liberty*, xiv.

152. George, *Life, Marriage, and Religious Liberty*, xiv. See George, "Barmen and the Baptists." George discusses with Mohler: Nazi Germany and the Baptist response, the background of social engagement by the church, and key issues regarding political involvement.

153. George, *Life, Marriage, and Religious Liberty*, xiv.

"our cherished confessional beliefs, this despite raucous criticism from some who claimed otherwise."[154]

George faced criticism from popular conservative Christian leaders such as R. C. Sproul,[155] Michael Horton,[156] and John MacArthur[157] when he joined with Catholics and Eastern Orthodox leaders among other denominations to sign *The Manhattan Declaration*.[158]

George defended the concentration of the declaration on the three specific issues chosen, when he said, "I have referred to these three issues as threshold issues. We go through these issues into a wider array of concern. But if we can't agree on the sanctity of life, the dignity of marriage, and religious freedom for all people then we really have no common ground on which to address these other issues."[159]

George referenced the important example of the Early Church in the matter of the sanctity of life:

> You have this image of the early Christians going through the trash heaps of Rome collecting the babies that have been abandoned and adopting them and nurturing them. The earliest document we have outside of the New Testament, the *Didache of the Twelve Apostles* says, 'Christians are those who will not practice abortion and infanticide.' This is a part of the DNA of what it means to be a follower of Jesus Christ.[160]

Conclusion

This chapter focused on the influence of George Huntston Williams on Timothy George's perspective of historical theology by providing a brief profile of Williams, from his early life to his career at Harvard Divinity School in Cambridge, Massachusetts. Next his major contributions were identified: church history as a theological discipline, ecumenism, and social

---

154. George, *Life, Marriage, and Religious Liberty*, xiv.
155. Sproul, "Manhattan Declaration," *Ligonier*.
156. Horton, "Review of *The Manhattan Declaration*," *White Horse Inn*.
157. MacArthur, "Manhattan Declaration," *Grace to You*.
158. George, "Manhattan Declaration." The first episode of the Beeson Divinity School podcast was George and Colson discussing the background and the purpose of *The Manhattan Declaration* a year after its announcement.
159. George, "Manhattan Declaration," 13:40–59.
160. George, "Manhattan Declaration," 15:16–40.

activism. These contributions influenced George's approach to historical theology in terms of his calling and work as a historical theologian in the following areas: history and doctrine, Evangelicals and Catholics Together (ECT), and *The Manhattan Declaration*.

In the same way that Williams viewed church history as a theological discipline, George integrated the study of history and doctrine. Just as Williams pioneered ecumenical cooperation between mainline Protestants and Roman Catholics, George led Evangelicals to join with Roman Catholics in theological and cultural engagement. As Williams was a historian who intervened in history through social activism, George joined with Catholics, Eastern Orthodox, and other Protestant leaders to declare *The Manhattan Declaration* and to take a stand against the cultural decay and loss of three threshold issues: sanctity of life, historic institution of marriage, and religious freedom. In sum, Williams contributed three main ingredients to George's life and ministry.

The influence of Williams is the first foundational piece to understanding George's approach to historical theology. Contributions from David Steinmetz in the history of biblical interpretation (chapter 4) and Jaroslav Pelikan in the study of Christian doctrine (chapter 5) will provide additional components of Timothy George's understanding of historical theology.

4

The Quest to Free the Church from Amnesia
David Steinmetz (1936-2015)

> We do not come to the study of the Bible alone but in the
> company of the whole people of God, the body of Christ
> scattered throughout time as well as space.
>
> —TIMOTHY GEORGE

Introduction

TIMOTHY GEORGE'S UNDERSTANDING OF historical theology and biblical exegesis builds on the work of David Steinmetz. This chapter offers a brief profile of Steinmetz's career and identifies his major contributions that influenced George's approach to historical theology in terms of his calling and work.

A brief biographical profile of Steinmetz's education and teaching career provides the context to focus on his historical and theological approach through contributions in historiography and biblical interpretation. George carried on the contributions of Steinmetz in his work as a historical theologian in two primary areas: Reformation studies and the history of biblical exegesis. George describes the achievements of Steinmetz's career by saying he was a committed churchman, a beloved teacher, and a pioneering scholar.¹ These descriptions provide the significant aspects of his career that will be examined.

Steinmetz is one of the three key figures that shaped Timothy George's understanding of historical theology, especially in the areas of Reformation studies and the history of biblical interpretation. The central question of this book, Timothy George's understanding of historical theology, has been established in terms of significance (chapter 1), biographical context (chapter 2), and the first key influencer George Huntston Williams (chapter 3). Now, chapter 4 examines the second of the three key influencers, David Steinmetz, who will be shown to shape George's understanding of historical theology in the areas of Reformation studies and the history of biblical exegesis.

Education and Career (1936–2015)

Education

David Steinmetz studied English at Wheaton College in Illinois, earning a bachelor of arts in 1958. He went to seminary at Drew University in New Jersey, earning a bachelor of divinity in 1961. He went on to do theological research at the University of Göttingen from 1964 until 1965. He wrote his dissertation under the supervision of Heiko Oberman at Harvard University, earning the doctor of theology in 1967. Timothy George describes Steinmetz's published dissertation *Misericordia Dei*[2] as a "superb appraisal of Staupitz and the medieval traditions on which he drew."[3]

Committed Churchman

David Steinmetz was ordained as a deacon by the Ohio Conference of the Methodist Church in Lakeside, Ohio, in 1959. He became an elder in the Methodist Church in 1961. Diarmaid MacCulloch describes Steinmetz as a "United Methodist minister who takes seriously his vocation to provide clergy and people with the tools to understand and profit from church history."[4]

---

1. George, "Remembering David Steinmetz's Quest."
2. Steinmetz, *Misericordia Dei*.
3. George, *Theology of the Reformers*, 52.
4. MacCulloch, Review of *Taking the Long View*, 563.

Timothy George said of Steinmetz's commitment level as a churchman: "He had a high view of the ordained ministry and encouraged young ministers to remain faithful, rather than original, in their preaching of the gospel."[5] In 1997 Steinmetz addressed students preparing for ministry in the Duke University Chapel. He charged the students, "The good news for the members of the graduating class who plan to enter the ordained ministry is that you don't have to invent your own gospel."[6] He clarified that while a congregation "hopes you will be imaginative and resourceful. It doesn't expect you to be original."[7] He explained the sense in which originality should be discouraged—"with respect to core convictions."[8] Steinmetz argued, "The church will authorize you to preach an ancient gospel you didn't cook up, and that is true whether you believe it or not."[9]

Steinmetz identified the main ingredient for successful ministry in the church. First, he said, "You will be commissioned by bishops and elders who have done it before you to preach the whole counsel of God, including the awkward bits we don't understand very well."[10] Second, he also addressed the alternative, a failure to minister faithfully. He clarified, "What you will not be ordained to do (though some of you will yield to the temptation to do it anyway) is to preach only those parts of the Christian tradition you have found personally meaningful."[11] Lastly, he argued that the minister must rely on the extensive wisdom of God's word for the people of God. He told the ministerial students, "God doesn't intend to mold the church in your image, you'll be relieved to know, but in the image of the crucified and risen Christ."[12]

Beloved Teacher

Steinmetz began his teaching career at Lancaster Theological Seminary where he taught for five years from 1966–71. He started teaching at Duke

---

5. George, "Remembering David Steinmetz's Quest."
6. Steinmetz, "For the Sake of the Gospel."
7. Steinmetz, "For the Sake of the Gospel."
8. Steinmetz, "For the Sake of the Gospel."
9. Steinmetz, "For the Sake of the Gospel."
10. Steinmetz, "For the Sake of the Gospel."
11. Steinmetz, "For the Sake of the Gospel."
12. Steinmetz, "For the Sake of the Gospel."

Retrieval for the Sake of Renewal

Divinity School in 1971.[13] Later, he served as the Amos Ragan Kearns Distinguished Professor of the History of Christianity. In 1986 Duke awarded Steinmetz as the University Scholar/Teacher of the Year. He also served as a visiting professor at three universities. First, in 1977 he taught at Harvard where he met Timothy George and served on his doctoral examination committee. Second, he taught at the University of Notre Dame in 1993, 1997, 2005, and 2008. Third, he taught at Emory University in 2010.

George said of Steinmetz as a teacher, "He was the best classroom teacher I have ever had."[14] His reason was that Steinmetz "was not only brilliant but also passionate and insightful."[15] He marveled at Steinmetz's abilities as a skillful instructor in the classroom who "never lost sight of the larger context of the texts and traditions he was so adept at bringing to life."[16]

George recalls examples of Steinmetz's passionate and insightful teaching. He remembers, "I shall never forget his early morning lectures in Andover Hall as he presented Calvin's life and thought like a great actor commanding the stage."[17] The impact of Steinmetz's teaching was that "no one dared miss his lively lectures—replete with chalk-drawn diagrams on the blackboard, lively interrogations of the 16th-century texts, and dramatic enactments of Reformation debates."[18] He describes the classroom experience with Steinmetz in terms of time travel. He wrote, "You felt like you were there with Luther and Zwingli at Marburg, with Calvin and Bolsec in Geneva."[19]

John Thompson notes how students characterized Steinmetz's instruction and teaching style as "fairness, detail, and good humor."[20] Thompson comments on Steinmetz as a mentor and doctoral supervisor, recalling the uncommon bonds of "collegiality and common purpose of a sort that would be hard to find elsewhere"[21] which Steinmetz's doctoral students formed with him.

---

13. See "David Steinmetz Dies at 79," para. 4.
14. George, "Remembering David Steinmetz's Quest," para. 4.
15. George, "Remembering David Steinmetz's Quest," para. 4.
16. George, "Remembering David Steinmetz's Quest," para. 4.
17. George, "Remembering David Steinmetz's Quest," para. 4.
18. George, "Remembering David Steinmetz's Quest," para. 4.
19. George, "Remembering David Steinmetz's Quest," para. 4.
20. "Remembering Leading Reformation Scholar," para. 2.
21. "Remembering Leading Reformation Scholar," para. 2.

Pioneering Scholar

In 1996 David Steinmetz was honored by his students with a Festschrift titled *Biblical Interpretation in the Era of the Reformation*.[22] Andreas Köstenberger reviewed the work and concluded, "This festschrift honoring the Reformation scholar David Steinmetz makes a significant contribution to the study of biblical interpretation during the Reformation period."[23] Elsie McKee describes this work as a "fitting tribute to David Steinmetz and to the field of exegetical history for which he has done so much."[24] Anthony Lane comments, "Steinmetz has been an important pioneer in the move towards viewing the exegesis of the Reformers not in splendid isolation but as part of an ongoing tradition."[25] In 2006 Steinmetz became a fellow of the American Academy of Arts and Sciences.[26] In 2010 the American Society of Church History recognized Steinmetz's achievements with the Distinguished Career Award.

Scott Manetsch praises Steinmetz as "one of our generation's most insightful interpreters of the sixteenth-century Reformation."[27] He says the achievement of Steinmetz was overcoming "the traditional divide between the Middle Ages and the early modern period."[28] It was by examining the intersection between the Middle Ages and the early Reformation period, Manetsch says, that Steinmetz discovered "the rich medieval inheritance that shaped Protestant theology and exegesis."[29] Diarmaid MacCulloch also comments, "David Steinmetz is one of our most distinguished Reformation historians, with an enviable track record of explaining the complexities of the period with elegant clarity."[30] In sum, Timothy George remarks, "Dr. Steinmetz was one of the great historians of the Reformation of our whole era."[31]

---

22. Muller and Thompson, *Biblical Interpretation*.
23. Köstenberger, Review of *Biblical Interpretation*, 107.
24. McKee, Review of *Biblical Interpretation*, 289.
25. Lane, Review of *Biblical Interpretation*, 158.
26. See "David Steinmetz Dies at 79," para. 3.
27. George, "In Honor of David Steinmetz," para. 6.
28. George, "In Honor of David Steinmetz," para. 6.
29. George, "In Honor of David Steinmetz," para. 6.
30. MacCulloch, Review of *Taking the Long View*, 563.
31. George, "Reformation as a Whole," 00:35–41.

Retrieval for the Sake of Renewal

Major Contributions from David Steinmetz

Historiography

Taking the Long View

David Steinmetz addressed the careful historical task and nature of historical theology: "All historical writing requires historians to 'go native.'"[32] By this phrase, Steinmetz meant that the historian should "learn the languages, the customs, the intellectual assumptions, and even the humor of the people they are studying."[33] He explained the unique challenge of going native for the Christian historian: "This is particularly true for historians of Christianity, who attempt to interpret a movement that adapts well to new cultures and has been adapting over and over again for two millennia."[34]

Steinmetz then moved from the question of how to understand the past to how to best communicate that meaning to those in the present: "Interpreters must interpret. They must explain to their readers in language and categories their readers can understand what they have learned from studying the writings and artifacts of an alien place and time."[35] He said, "What they are not allowed to do is correct the opinions of the past or reclothe long-dead figures in the fashions of the present."[36] He did not believe that the figures and the events of the past should be adjusted. Instead, he desired to make these historical riches accessible for contemporary theology.

Steinmetz did not separate the historical and theological tasks, but he did distinguish them and want to uphold each distinctive role. He understood the urgent need to recover the past. He said, "Their task as historians is to enable the voices of Christians from distant ages to be heard again by a church that may have forgotten them and desperately needs to hear them again."[37] He also understood the obligation to evaluate the past as a theological task to address the present. Thus, he clarified, "This does not mean that historians of Christianity have been deprived of the right to make normative judgments about the past—only that they must make those judgments as theologians, speaking constructively to the church, rather than

---

32. Steinmetz, *Taking the Long View*, 148.
33. Steinmetz, *Taking the Long View*, 148.
34. Steinmetz, *Taking the Long View*, 148.
35. Steinmetz, *Taking the Long View*, 148.
36. Steinmetz, *Taking the Long View*, 149.
37. Steinmetz, *Taking the Long View*, 149.

as historians, clarifying what was once believed and taught."[38] He aimed to uphold the historian's craft of investigating the past with the theologian's calling to instruct the church.

Steinmetz addressed the attitude and care in which the historian should operate. He wrote, "In short, historians must be methodologically humble, even if they are not humble in any other way. They must accept the past on its terms rather than on their own."[39] He argued that a "critical reading of the Christian past, born of genuine affection for it, still challenges the church to remember its past and, by doing so, take the long view on its present."[40]

The Necessity of the Past

In 1976 David Steinmetz wrote the article "The Necessity of the Past"[41] in *Theology Today*. Diarmaid MacCulloch describes this work as "a wonderful essay . . . on the value of history to the practice of Christianity."[42] First, Steinmetz established the nature and fundamental purpose of memory: "Memory is a faculty that takes some aspect of the past and makes it a datum of my present, as real and tangible as the pew on which I am sitting or the neighbor who is seated beside me. Memory grasps the past and makes it a part of my present."[43] Next, he observed an essential relationship between memory and the ability to live rightly in the present: "It does so because I need that past in order to function in the present. It is for the sake of the present that memory lays hold of the events of the past."[44] Third, he offered the central doctrine and event of Christianity as an example: "Christian faith is based on certain remembered events in history—above all, on the resurrection of Jesus Christ from the dead."[45]

Steinmetz argued for the importance of history on the basis that Christianity does not fundamentally depend on philosophical or ethical ideas. It does, however, depend on historical events: "From the standpoint

---

38. Steinmetz, *Taking the Long View*, 149.
39. Steinmetz, *Taking the Long View*, 149.
40. Steinmetz, *Taking the Long View*, 156.
41. Steinmetz, "Necessity of the Past," 168–77.
42. MacCulloch, Review of *Taking the Long View*, 563.
43. Steinmetz, "Necessity of the Past," 171.
44. Steinmetz, "Necessity of the Past," 171.
45. Steinmetz, "Necessity of the Past," 171.

of the Christian faith, the importance of Jesus of Nazareth is not that he uttered the Golden Rule, but that he was conceived, born, suffered, crucified, died, buried, and rose."[46] He draws out the implication that "my faith as a Christian is inextricably bound up with those events of the past."[47] Therefore, for Steinmetz, "To be a Christian is by definition to be involved in the past, if only for the sake of the present and future."[48]

Steinmetz believed that there was both a benefit that came with an awareness of the past and a cost in avoiding it: "Church history helps us become self-conscious concerning our dependence on the traditions of the past."[49] Reliance on the past, however, does not mean uncritical acceptance of it. He instead believed this realization "gives us the freedom, when necessary, to become critical of those traditions."[50] He argued the opposite: "People who believe that they have no creed except the Bible will, I am sorry to say, be victimized by the past."[51] It is the attempt to be independent of the past that results in a type of slavery of ignorance rather than leading to the freedom to engage with the past both charitably and critically.

Steinmetz commented on the notion of the past influencing the church in the present, saying, "I do not think that it is a bad thing for the Christian church in the present to be influenced by the church of the past in its understanding of the Christian faith."[52] He insisted, "Quite the contrary: it is not only inevitable that the church in the present will be influenced by the past, it is even desirable."[53] Therefore, he gave this charge: "What is intolerable in a Christian theologian or pastor is a lack of awareness of that influence."[54] Thus, the Christian leader must be aware of the effects of the past on the Christian community.

Steinmetz examined the positive and negative consequences of tradition. He suggested desirable results of tradition: "Christians may be under the influence of traditions that lead them into a faithful apprehension of the Gospel and that provide reliable guidelines for responsible action in

---

46. Steinmetz, "Necessity of the Past," 172.
47. Steinmetz, "Necessity of the Past," 172.
48. Steinmetz, "Necessity of the Past," 172.
49. Steinmetz, "Necessity of the Past," 173.
50. Steinmetz, "Necessity of the Past," 173.
51. Steinmetz, "Necessity of the Past," 173.
52. Steinmetz, "Necessity of the Past," 173.
53. Steinmetz, "Necessity of the Past," 173.
54. Steinmetz, "Necessity of the Past," 173.

the present."[55] He also contended there might be undesirable results of tradition when he said, "but they may also be misled and misguided by tradition."[56] He warned, "As long as they accept uncritically what they have received from the past, they put ourselves unreservedly in its power. Tradition can obscure as well as clarify the Gospel."[57]

Steinmetz, however, argued for the necessity of studying the past to overcome the adverse effects of tradition: "The study of history gives the church freedom vis-à-vis its past: freedom to appropriate its past wisdom, when it can, and overcome its faithlessness and sin, when it must."[58] Therefore, Steinmetz, while admitting the problems in the past, still demonstrated its necessity.

The central purpose of church history as a theological discipline according to Steinmetz is understood by identifying its recipient, its scope, and its result: "The aim of church history as a theological discipline is to provide the church with a more universal and self-critical perspective within which to make responsible theological and pastoral decisions in the present."[59] First, the intended recipient is not primarily the academy but "the church."[60] Second, the scope is both a "more universal and self-critical perspective."[61] Third, the result is to "make responsible theological and pastoral decisions."[62]

The study of church history, for Steinmetz, should result in an acceptance of the development of doctrine and encourage an ecclesial humility. He claimed, "Church history has an indispensable role to play as a theological stimulus and corrective."[63] For instance, he said, "In freeing Christians from theological parochialism, it also results in a loss of innocence."[64] He went on to explain, "Students see how the traditions they learned in a parish or parachurch group evolved over the course of the centuries and discover, sometimes to their chagrin, that their tradition, whatever else it may

---

55. Steinmetz, "Necessity of the Past," 173.
56. Steinmetz, "Necessity of the Past," 173.
57. Steinmetz, "Necessity of the Past," 173.
58. Steinmetz, "Necessity of the Past," 173.
59. Steinmetz, "Necessity of the Past," 173.
60. Steinmetz, "Necessity of the Past," 173.
61. Steinmetz, "Necessity of the Past," 173.
62. Steinmetz, "Necessity of the Past," 173.
63. Steinmetz, "Necessity of the Past," 173.
64. Steinmetz, "Necessity of the Past," 174.

be, is not simply a repristination in the twenty-first century of the primitive apostolic faith."[65] It is when students realize that their contemporary tradition is not the same in all aspects as the first Christians that they can begin to understand them and their tradition better.

The study of church history provides the right context to understand different denominations and Christian traditions. Steinmetz observed the experience of students: "As they become acquainted with traditions other than their own, they are painfully disabused of the idea that tradition A (their own) is the only possible option that the church has followed or, indeed, can follow. When they place tradition A alongside traditions B, C, and D, they realize for the first time what tradition A really is."[66] As a result, he believed that theologians could, through studying church history, "become aware of the diversity of traditions in the Christian church and self-critical of their own tradition."[67]

For Steinmetz, historical theology should result in an ecumenical perspective and requires a humble attitude: "The first task of church history as a theological discipline is to free Christians from their own parochialism and make them truly catholic. The study of church history also teaches Christians to make modest claims for their theology. There is a sense in which theology is a humble science."[68] Thus, he expected the student of church history to gain more perspective and less pride.

The benefit of studying the past is dependent on using the right methods. Steinmetz explained, "We study the past because it is able to instruct us, if we learn to ask it the right questions and discover how to engage it on its own terms."[69] He viewed the effort involved in learning from the past as worthwhile: "It opens us to insights, ideas, and questions we would have encountered in no other way."[70]

The Quest to Free the Church from Amnesia

Steinmetz made a striking comparison between the effect of amnesia on people and the condition of the church. He began by explaining how people

65. Steinmetz, "Necessity of the Past," 173–74.
66. Steinmetz, "Necessity of the Past," 174.
67. Steinmetz, "Necessity of the Past," 174.
68. Steinmetz, "Necessity of the Past," 174.
69. Steinmetz, "Necessity of the Past," 174.
70. Steinmetz, "Necessity of the Past," 176.

who suffer from amnesia not only lose the past but also become disoriented in the present and the future. He said, "People who have lost their memories can no longer remember who they are. That means that they can no longer function effectively in the present and have no secure plans for the future. They have lost their past, and that has emptied their present of meaning and clouded their future."[71] He concluded, "We must have contact with the past, if only for the sake of the present and the future."[72]

Steinmetz argued that memory also functions in the same way in the life of the church: "The church could, I suppose, lose its memory as well. It is certainly tempted to do that often enough. But a church that has lost its memory of the past can only wander about aimlessly in the present and despair of its future. The church needs the past, if only for the sake of the present and the future."[73]

Steinmetz argued that the study of the past is essential for faithful obedience to God in the present. He anticipated misconceptions about the discipline of historical theology: "The invitation to study the history of the church is not an irrelevant call to forsake the mission of the church and to lose oneself in a past no longer recoverable."[74] Next, he explains the implications for the church when he says, "It is, rather, a call to abandon peripheral matters, to put an end to aimless meanderings and nervous activism, to learn once again who we are and to whom we belong."[75] Therefore, the church's memory is necessary for the fulfillment of the church's mission. Steinmetz concluded, "Only when we have regained our identity from the past can we undertake our mission in the present."[76]

Doing History as Theologians

In 2015 David Steinmetz wrote the article "Doing History as Theologians."[77] He claimed that church history had the potential "to clarify the situation of the church at the present time."[78] He was making a claim about the

---

71. Steinmetz, "Necessity of the Past," 176.
72. Steinmetz, "Necessity of the Past," 176.
73. Steinmetz, "Necessity of the Past," 176.
74. Steinmetz, "Necessity of the Past," 176.
75. Steinmetz, "Necessity of the Past," 176.
76. Steinmetz, "Necessity of the Past," 176.
77. Steinmetz, "Doing History as Theologians," 174–80.
78. Steinmetz, "Doing History as Theologians," 180.

possibilities of history related to the field of theology: "History can illuminate our theological task."[79] He believed it could only be done under three conditions. The first condition is interpreting the history "on its own terms and not on ours, accepting the past as it was and not as we might wish it to be."[80] The second condition necessary is discovering the historical situation. The historical context according to Steinmetz is made up of the "intellectual boundaries (language, setting, and philosophical presuppositions) that separate us from a different and often alien place and time."[81] The third condition is learning to "translate as clearly as we can what we have discovered from our research in a past world in which we have never lived."[82] He concluded that "only by proceeding in this way can we learn to do history as an essential theological task."[83]

Biblical Interpretation

Pre-Critical Exegesis

In 1980 David Steinmetz published the article "The Superiority of Pre-Critical Exegesis."[84] Scott Manetsch applauds his article as a "forceful defense of 'pre-critical' biblical exegesis [that] will no doubt continue to serve as inspiration for scholars studying the history of biblical interpretation and its relevance for the church today."[85]

George writes, "A leading scholar of the Reformation, Steinmetz does not deal directly with sixteenth-century exegesis in this article. Rather, he tackles what C. S. Lewis once called the 'chronological snobbery' of scholarly methods that dismiss Reformation-era studies of the Bible, along with the interpretive tradition that preceded them, as antiquated, regressive, and all but useless for understanding the Bible today."[86] Malcom Yarnell agrees:

79. Steinmetz, "Doing History as Theologians," 180.
80. Steinmetz, "Doing History as Theologians," 180.
81. Steinmetz, "Doing History as Theologians," 181.
82. Steinmetz, "Doing History as Theologians," 181.
83. Steinmetz, "Doing History as Theologians," 181.
84. Steinmetz, "Superiority of Pre-Critical Exegesis," 27–38. For a recent evaluation of Steinmetz's thesis see Treier, "Superiority of Pre-Critical Exegesis?," 77–103.
85. George, "In Honor of David Steinmetz," para. 6.
86. George, *Reading Scripture with the Reformers*, 26–27; See Steinmetz, *Taking the Long View*, 169. Steinmetz comments, "For a brief survey of medieval hermeneutical theory that takes into account recent historical research see James S. Preus, *From Shadow*

The Quest to Free the Church from Amnesia

"It is a peculiarly modernist hubris, a conceit rooted in its mythology of progress, to consider the contributions of modern scholars to the theological conversation superior, whether as exegetes or as philosophers, to those of another period."[87]

George evaluates Steinmetz's achievement. First, he understands it is as a return "to Augustine and the early church."[88] Second, he recognizes that Steinmetz traces "how the famous theory of the fourfold sense of Scripture came to be widely used in the Middle Ages." Third, he believes that Steinmetz's approach seeks to take "seriously the words and sayings of Scripture, including implicit meanings beyond the original intentions of the human authors."[89]

George does clarify and acknowledge "the loaded terms 'precritical' and 'superior.'"[90] He is concerned that "the concept of precritical exegesis" can be "fraught with hubris and condescension."[91] He insists that precritical interpreters were not naive to the challenges of biblical interpretation: "A close reading of premodern exegesis will show that many of its practitioners were keenly aware of the kind of issues that preoccupy contemporary students of the Bible such as the authorship of the Pentateuch, multiple versions of the same event, imprecision in quotations, the so-called synoptic problem, and so forth."[92]

On the one hand, Steinmetz uses the work of Benjamin Jowett to represent the modern approach and values in biblical interpretation. He quotes Benjamin Jowett, saying, "The true use of interpretation is to get rid of interpretation, and leave us alone in company with the author."[93] Timothy George points out how Alexander Campbell instructed his followers "to open the New Testament as if mortal man had never seen it before."[94] On the other hand, Steinmetz wrote, "I am inclined to agree with C. S. Lewis, who

---

to Promise (Cambridge, MA: Harvard University Press, 1969), 9–149."

87. Yarnell, *Formation of Christian Doctrine*, 2.
88. George, *Reading Scripture with the Reformers*, 27.
89. George, *Reading Scripture with the Reformers*, 27.
90. George, *Reading Scripture with the Reformers*, 30.
91. George, *Reading Scripture with the Reformers*, 30.
92. George, *Reading Scripture with the Reformers*, 30.
93. Jowett, "On the Interpretation of Scripture," 384.
94. Cited in Hatch, "Sola Scriptura and Novus Ordo Seclorum," 72.

commented on his own book *Till We Have Faces*: "An author doesn't necessarily understand the meaning of his own story better than anyone else."[95]

Douglas Sweeney comments on Steinmetz's contribution to the study of biblical interpretation: "As David Steinmetz and his students have made clear in recent years, the Protestant reformers packed a lot of what had formerly passed as 'spiritual' understanding into their 'literal' exegesis. They did not intend to reinvent the reading of the Bible in a modern, critical way."[96] Sweeney points out how Steinmetz remarked about the Reformers: "They advocated . . . a letter pregnant with spiritual significance, a letter big-bellied with meaning formerly relegated by the quadriga to allegory or tropology."[97] Sweeney acknowledges the many students and the influence that Steinmetz has had in the field of historical studies and biblical interpretation when he refers to "the Steinmetz school."[98]

Luther in Context

In 1986 David Steinmetz wrote *Luther in Context*.[99] James Nestingen comments on the wider achievement of the work saying, "Steinmetz represents a generation of American Luther scholars who have come into their own."[100] Terry Thomas describes Steinmetz's unique contribution in this work when he wrote, "While Luther interpreters sometimes specialize in Luther's biography or his polemical treatises, Steinmetz focuses on Luther's interpretation of the Bible, and this comes through in each chapter."[101] Thomas acknowledges, "The book not only brings to the surface well-known Luther themes, but explores Luther's relationship to other medieval and sixteenth-century theologians."[102] Steinmetz's essays on Luther focus on his biblical exegesis in comparison with other contemporaries in his historical context.

---

95. Steinmetz, "Superiority of Pre-Critical Exegesis," 36. Steinmetz quotes Lewis, *Letters of C. S. Lewis*, 273.

96. Sweeney, *Edwards the Exegete*, 46.

97. Steinmetz, "Divided by a Common Past," 249.

98. Sweeney, *Edwards the Exegete*, 291.

99. Steinmetz, *Luther in Context*.

100. Nestingen, Review of *Luther in Context*, 305.

101. Thomas, Review of *Luther in Context*, 282.

102. Thomas, Review of *Luther in Context*, 282.

The Quest to Free the Church from Amnesia

Calvin in Context

In 1995 David Steinmetz wrote *Calvin in Context*.[103] Richard Mouw describes the focus of these essays as examining Calvin's "patterns of biblical exegesis."[104] The work focuses on comparative theology in historical context. Mark Edwards of St. Olaf College commends the work by saying, "If I wanted my students to see Calvin within his larger theological context there is no better guide than Steinmetz's volume."[105] Edwards explains:

> Steinmetz facilitates these comparisons by frequently framing the topic at hand as a question of exegesis of particular texts of Scripture. In this way, Steinmetz has a ready means of comparison. How, he asks, did Calvin deal with a particular passage in Scripture, and how did Calvin's sources or Calvin's contemporaries deal with the same passage?[106]

Thus, the work is an examination of the exegetical tradition at the time of the Reformation.

Donald McKim commends the work when he says, "Steinmetz uses an immense range of primary sources and places Calvin's interpretive decisions clearly within the setting of other biblical commentators."[107] McKim says this work does not attempt to provide a general account of Calvin's historical context but instead offers the specifics of "a dynamic interaction with those who were commenting on the same exegetical and theological issues."[108]

Steinmetz explains the argument and goal of the book: "The best and most productive way to study Calvin is to place him in the context of the theological and exegetical traditions that formed him and in the lively company of the friends and enemies from whom he learned and with whom he quarreled."[109]

---

103. Steinmetz, *Calvin in Context*.
104. Mouw, Review of *Calvin in Context*, 370.
105. Edwards, Review of *Calvin in Context*, 628.
106. Edwards, Review of *Calvin in Context*, 628.
107. McKim, Review of *Calvin in Context*, 349.
108. McKim, Review of *Calvin in Context*, 349.
109. Steinmetz, *Calvin in Context*, 278.

Retrieval for the Sake of Renewal

Reception and Transmission by Timothy George

Reformation Studies

Timothy George recalls when he was a student of Steinmetz, saying, "I took his class on 'Calvin and the Reformed Tradition,' the same course he himself had once taken with Oberman."[110] George himself later taught the course at Beeson Divinity School.[111]

David Dockery notes the influence that Steinmetz and others had on George's Reformation studies: "Through his study of the Reformers and his studies with premier scholars like George Huntston Williams, Heiko Oberman, and David Steinmetz, George developed a deep appreciation for the role of the Word of God across the ages."[112] George also describes the Reformation as a "movement with a long view of history,"[113] borrowing terminology from Steinmetz's writing.

In 1987 Timothy George wrote in the preface to the first edition of *Theology of the Reformers* an acknowledgement to the history and theology professors with whom he had studied the Reformation when he said, "I would like to mention those scholars with whom I have studied Reformation history and theology."[114] He first mentions his undergraduate history professor from the University of Tennessee at Chattanooga, William J. Wright. He then mentions his professors from his graduate and doctoral studies at Harvard University such as "James S. Preus, Arthur C. McGill, Caroline Walker Bynum, Donald R. Kelly, David C. Steinmetz, Ian D. K. Siggins, Heiko A. Oberman, John E. Booty, Peter J. Gomes, and last, but not least, George Huntston Williams."[115] He writes about his professors, "To each of these I owe much more than a prefatory acknowledgment can

---

110. George, "In Honor of David Steinmetz," para. 2.

111. See Beeson Divinity School, "Curriculum," 44. For the course description titled Calvin and the Reformed Tradition: "This course studies the life and theology of John Calvin. Attention focuses on Calvin's role in the development of Reformed Protestantism as well as his distinctive contribution to Reformation theology. Readings include selections from Calvin's commentaries, letters, polemical and theological treatises and Institutes."

112. Dockery, "Timothy George," 7.

113. George, "What the Reformers Thought They Were Doing," 25.

114. George, *Theology of the Reformers*, 7.

115. George, *Theology of the Reformers*, 7.

express."[116] George also invited and hosted Steinmetz for the Reformation Heritage Series lectures at Beeson Divinity School in 1995.[117]

The History of Biblical Exegesis

Timothy George credits David Steinmetz with helping scholars "see the interpretive tradition of the church not as a problem to be overcome, but rather as an indispensable aid for rightly understanding the inspired Word."[118] For example, George remembers, "Steinmetz once said in my hearing, *sola Scriptura* does not mean *nuda Scriptura* but rather *prima Scriptura*—not Scripture only but Scripture as the norm by which all other writings and teachings are judged."[119] Under George's leadership, Beeson Divinity School offered the course titled, "History of Biblical Interpretation."[120]

George clarifies the intent of Steinmetz's project to retrieve the premodern exegetical tradition: "The appeal to the superiority of premodern biblical exegesis is a protest against the reductionism inherent in the longstanding monopoly of the historical-critical method, not a rejection of rigorous historical study of the Bible."[121] He admits the shortcomings of the tradition saying, "Biblical commentaries written in the sixteenth century are marked by diverse and sometimes clashing interpretations, to say nothing of the many centuries of Christian exegesis that preceded them."[122] He addresses the advantages of premodern exegesis when he writes, "What this tradition shares in common, often in contrast to more recent critical approaches, are five principles that guide our reading and understanding of Scripture."[123]

George identifies these five principles from the precritical tradition. First, he begins with the foundation that the Bible is the "inspired and

---

116. George, *Theology of the Reformers*, 7.
117. Steinmetz, "Reformation in Context."
118. George, "Remembering David Steinmetz's Quest."
119. George, "Remembering David Steinmetz's Quest."
120. Beeson Divinity School, *Beeson Bulletin 2019-2020*, 44. The course description says, "This course covers the history of interpretation of Scripture from New Testament times to the present. Special attention is given to doctrinal issues, and cases are illustrated from specific biblical texts."
121. George, *Reading Scripture with the Reformers*, 31.
122. George, *Reading Scripture with the Reformers*, 31.
123. George, *Reading Scripture with the Reformers*, 31.

authoritative Word of God."[124] Second, it should be understood through the "the rule of faith."[125] Third, it should be interpreted through a "trinitarian hermeneutic."[126] Fourth, it must be central and visible in "the worship of the church."[127] Fifth, studying it is a "means of grace."[128]

George expresses his high view of the Holy Bible and the role of historical theology in its interpretation: "If we are to take this word seriously we must engage simultaneously in a threefold hermeneutical move."[129] He states that the first hermeneutical move must address "what it meant in its original setting."[130] He categorizes this step in the process of determining the meaning of a text as the "special task of *Old and New Testament study*."[131] The second hermeneutical move according to George is to investigate "what it means today."[132] He understands this as the "combined task of biblical, systematic, and practical theology."[133] The third hermeneutical move focuses on "what it has meant throughout the vast continuum of the Christian experience."[134] He claims that this question regarding the history of biblical exegesis is the "special task of historical theology."[135] Just as Gerhard Ebeling claimed, "Church history is the history of the exposition of Scripture."[136]

George reflects on the link between his work as the General Editor of the *Reformation Commentary on Scripture* and the work of Steinmetz: "The RCS [Reformation Commentary on Scripture] would not have been possible without the pioneering work of Steinmetz."[137] John L. Thompson served on the Reformation Commentary Series advisory board and was one of Steinmetz's students. Thompson comments on the continuing influence of Steinmetz: "As one of this generation's pioneers in reviving the study of

124. George, *Reading Scripture with the Reformers*, 31.
125. George, *Reading Scripture with the Reformers*, 32.
126. George, *Reading Scripture with the Reformers*, 34.
127. George, *Reading Scripture with the Reformers*, 35.
128. George, *Reading Scripture with the Reformers*, 36.
129. George, "Dogma beyond Anathema," 701.
130. George, "Dogma beyond Anathema," 701.
131. George, "Dogma beyond Anathema," 701.
132. George, "Dogma beyond Anathema," 701.
133. George, "Dogma beyond Anathema," 701.
134. George, "Dogma beyond Anathema," 701.
135. George, "Dogma beyond Anathema," 701.
136. Ebeling, *Word of God and Tradition*, 11.
137. George, "Remembering Leading Reformation Scholar," para. 4.

the history of exegesis, David Steinmetz set a sterling example of careful scholarship, attention to historical context, resistance to easy stereotyping, and respect for the formative influence of Christian history for the church today."[138]

George instructs, "We do not come to the study of the Bible alone but in the company of the whole people of God, the body of Christ scattered throughout time as well as space."[139] He explains, "It will not suffice merely to have our New Testament in one hand, and the latest word from current biblical scholarship (even if it comes from our favorite evangelical press!) in the other. We must also learn to 'read alongside' the church fathers, reformers, and theologians of ages past."[140]

George cautions against accepting the exegetical tradition of the church without careful evaluation: "None of their interpretations is inerrant, and we must subject them all along with our own—to the divine touchstone of Holy Scripture itself."[141] He still encourages engagement with the exegetical tradition on the basis of the continuing activity of the Holy Spirit saying, "Still, the Holy Spirit did not abandon the church with the death of the apostles."[142] Therefore, according to George, if contemporary Christians want to "prayerfully listen for what the Spirit is saying to us today, we will do well to heed what he has been saying to the people of God throughout the history of the church."[143] He concludes, "The massive consensus of thoughtful Christian interpretation of the Word down the ages (and on most matters of importance there is such a thing) is not likely to be wrong."[144]

George argues for the important role of community in biblical interpretation. He rejects an individualistic approach to biblical interpretation as the "Enlightenment model of the Bible student as a Lone Ranger, out on his own away from the church,"[145] which, he warns, "inevitably leads to distorted, if not heretical, conclusions."[146] Instead, he argues, "A renewed

---

138. "Remembering Leading Reformation Scholar," para. 2.
139. George, "Profiles of Expository Preaching," 90.
140. George, "What We Mean," para. 15.
141. George, "What We Mean," para. 15.
142. George, "What We Mean," para. 15.
143. George, "What We Mean," para. 15.
144. George, "What We Mean," para. 15.
145. George, "What We Mean," para. 16.
146. George, "What We Mean," para. 16.

appreciation of the Bible as the book of the church should make us more aware of our need to explore it in and with, rather than without and apart from, the larger Christian fellowship."[147]

Conclusion

David Steinmetz made significant contributions to Timothy George's understanding of historical theology through his writings in the historiography of historical theology as well as offering the foundation for and multiple works in the history of biblical interpretation. This chapter offered a brief sketch of Steinmetz's teaching career and scholarship, and it identified the major contributions that influenced George's approach to historical theology.

George carried on the contributions of Steinmetz in his work as a historical theologian in the areas of Reformation studies and the history of biblical exegesis. He looked to Steinmetz as an example of a committed churchman, a beloved teacher, and a scholar.[148] The central question of this book, Timothy George's understanding of historical theology, has been established in terms of significance (chapter 1), biographical context (chapter 2), and the first key influencer, George Huntston Williams (chapter 3). Chapter 4 has examined the second of the three key influencers, David Steinmetz. Contributions from Jaroslav Pelikan in the study of Christian doctrine (chapter 5) will provide additional components of George's understanding of historical theology.

---

147. George, "What We Mean," para. 16.
148. George, "Remembering David Steinmetz's Quest."

5

Delighted by Doctrine
Jaroslav Pelikan (1923–2006)

> I never had Jaroslav Pelikan as a classroom teacher, but I was one of his students, as everyone seriously interested in Christian history has to be.
>
> —TIMOTHY GEORGE

Introduction

Timothy George's understanding of historical theology, both its methodology and its model, is influenced by the work of Jaroslav Pelikan. This chapter offers a brief profile of Pelikan's career and identifies his major contributions that influenced George's approach to historical theology through Pelikan's methodology, major works of historical theology, and his definition of Christian doctrine.

A brief biographical profile of Pelikan's education and teaching career provides insight into his historical and theological approach as well as his contributions to the study of Christian doctrine and Christian Creeds. George carried on the contributions of Pelikan in his work as a historical theologian in two primary areas: the *meaning* of Christian doctrine and the *value* of Christian Creeds.

Pelikan is one of the three key figures that shaped George's understanding of historical theology, especially in the areas of theological studies and the historical method. The central question of this book, George's understanding of historical theology, has been established in terms of significance (chapter 1), biographical context (chapter 2); the first key influencer, George Huntston Williams (chapter 3); and the second key influencer, David Steinmetz (chapter 4). Chapter 5 examines the last of the three key influencers, Jaroslav Pelikan, who will be shown to shape Timothy George's understanding of historical theology through the methodology of his historical-theological scholarship, his major works in the field, and his understanding of Christian doctrine.

Education and Career (1923–2006)

Slavic Heritage

Jaroslav Pelikan's education began at home. Pelikan recalled, "I like to say that I was born into a family that was rich in everything except money—good food in abundance, music, books, languages, and above all tradition and faith."[1] He viewed his parents as "my first teachers of theology."[2] At home his parents used resources such as Luther's Small Catechism, Lutheran chorales, and many books from his father's library.[3] Timothy George comments, "Pelikan's deep religious faith was nurtured on Luther's Small Catechism, the great chorales of J. S. Bach, and, above all, the Bible. Each of these—Luther, Bach, and the Bible—would play a major role in his scholarly work."[4]

George points to a link between the realization of Pelikan's career and the foundation of his home life: "Pelikan's remarkable scholarly career was rooted in his Slavic family background."[5] Zoe Ingalls of the *Chronicle of Higher Education* reported about Pelikan that "he knew from an early age that he wanted to be a scholar. And he made the decision early on what the focus of his scholarship would be."[6] Kenneth Briggs reported about the direction of Pelikan's early life, saying, "He knew his ambition was to study theology."[7] Pelikan remembered about his childhood, "I could not reach

1. Pelikan, "Personal Memoir," 31.
2. Pelikan, "Personal Memoir," 32.
3. Pelikan, "Personal Memoir," 32.
4. George, "Delighted by Doctrine," 43–45.
5. George, "Delighted by Doctrine," 43–45.
6. Ingalls, "Yale's Jaroslav Pelikan," 4.
7. Briggs, "Linguistics Are the Key."

the dining room table, my parents had me sit on volumes of the *Patrologia*, with the result that I absorbed the church fathers *a posteriori*."[8]

George wrote about Pelikan's gift with linguistics: "His facility with languages was astounding—not only the classical tongues of Greek, Latin, and Hebrew, but also German, Slovak, Czech, Dutch, Russian, Serbian, all the romance languages, and many more."[9] He gave an example of Pelikan's unusual gift with languages: "On occasion he would stay up late at night listening to a shortwave radio to keep fresh his language skills—including Albanian, which he once found useful in a conversation with a taxi driver."[10]

Education

In 1942 Jaroslav Pelikan went to study at Concordia Seminary in St. Louis, Missouri. He remembered, "Going on to the seminary was a natural step in 1942, even though it was generally recognized, especially by my parents, that my vocation lay in scholarship and teaching rather than in the pastoral ministry."[11] He went to seminary to become a professor, not a pastor.

Pelikan reflected on what he gained during his time at Concordia Seminary: "Above all, my student years at Concordia Seminary gave me what confessional Lutheranism could have been expected to give, a detailed knowledge and technical grasp of church doctrine."[12] He specifically focused on two central dogmas or doctrines. The first doctrine was the Trinity. He conceded that the "instruction was (only in its Western configuration, to be sure)."[13] The second doctrine was the "two natures in Christ (which, because of its controversies with Calvinism over the doctrine of the real presence in the Eucharist, sixteenth- and seventeenth-century Lutheranism had elaborated largely on the basis of the Greek church fathers and later councils)."[14]

Pelikan's calling to focus on the history of Christian doctrine became clearer to him during his time studying at Concordia Seminary: "Despite occasional twinges of an inclination toward systematic theology or

8. Pelikan, "Personal Memoir," 32.
9. George, "Delighted by Doctrine," 203.
10. George, "Delighted by Doctrine," 203.
11. Pelikan, "Personal Memoir," 31.
12. Pelikan, "Personal Memoir," 35.
13. Pelikan, "Personal Memoir," 35.
14. Pelikan, "Personal Memoir," 35.

dogmatics, however, I knew that it was the history of Christian doctrine, more usually called (from its German origins and career as *Dogmengeschichte*) 'the history of dogma,' that I wanted to study and for which this combination of preparatory studies had in a special way been equipping me."[15] Therefore, his time studying a variety of subjects at Concordia Seminary confirmed his calling to study the history of doctrine.

In 1944 Pelikan recalled, "I really hit my stride only in the autumn of 1944, when I entered the Ph.D. program of the Divinity School of the University of Chicago."[16] Pelikan was motivated to attend this school not only because of its academic prestige and the ability to stay with his parents but most important to him was the opportunity to study the history of Christianity under Matthew Spinka and Wilhelm Pauck.[17]

Originally, Pelikan wanted to write a dissertation with Spinka, who was a specialist in Slavic Christianity, and with Pauck, who was a specialist on the Reformation. When he arrived at the University of Chicago, Spinka was no longer there so Pauck became his supervisor. Pelikan later wrote a tribute to Pauck in the work *Interpreters of Luther*.[18]

Career

In 1946 Jaroslav Pelikan began his academic career at Valparaiso University in Indiana. Pelikan remembered, "My first academic appointment was in a department of history (as would my final appointment be)."[19] He was appointed as an Assistant Professor. He stated, "At Valparaiso University from 1946 to 1949 I taught a variety of courses in European history, with a concentration on intellectual history, including philosophy, but I did not have the opportunity to teach the history of Christian thought."[20]

In 1949 Concordia Seminary hired Pelikan to teach the history of Christian thought. He moved to St. Louis, Missouri, where he became a junior faculty member. He recalled, "I took over the existing course in 'History of Dogma,' which concluded with the Reformation, and added a course

---

15. Pelikan, "Personal Memoir," 35.
16. Pelikan, "Personal Memoir," 35.
17. Pelikan, "Personal Memoir," 36.
18. Pelikan, "Wilhelm Pauck," 1–8.
19. Pelikan, "Personal Memoir," 37.
20. Pelikan, "Personal Memoir," 37.

on the history of theology since the Reformation."[21] He was returning to the seminary where he previously studied Christian doctrine to teach it.

In 1953 Pelikan returned to the University of Chicago. He wrote, "I accepted the invitation of the University of Chicago to succeed my mentor Wilhelm Pauck, who had meanwhile accepted the Briggs Chair of Church History at Union Theological Seminary in New York."[22] In 1959 he earned a promotion to the rank of full professorship in historical theology.

Although Pelikan was a teacher, he was also determined to be a life-long student of the Christian Tradition. He explained, "For the next nine years at Chicago I gave a year-long lecture course 'The History of Christian Thought,' usually with an accompanying seminar each quarter on specific topics from across all the periods of the history."[23] He spoke of teaching in terms of "carrying on my private education in public, filling in gaps from my previous study and deepening my grasp of the larger history."[24]

In 1962 Pelikan became the Titus Street Professor of Ecclesiastical History at Yale Divinity School. He wrote, "When I moved to Yale in 1962, it was to succeed Roland H. Bainton in the Titus Street Professorship of Ecclesiastical History in the Yale Divinity School, but with the understanding that I would take over Robert Lowry Calhoun's sequence on 'The History of Christian Doctrine.'"[25]

Pelikan said about his teaching, "My signature course in Yale College was a two-semester sequence on 'The Intellectual History of the Middle Ages East and West,' from the Cappadocians and Augustine to the Renaissance and the fall of Constantinople."[26] Pelikan recalled his signature teaching style: "Students and colleagues used to complain that when I was expounding Augustine they thought I was a card-carrying Augustinian, until I came to John of Damascus or Thomas Aquinas or Luther or Schleiermacher or Dostoevsky, when I was again stating the position of each of them as though from within."[27] He taught with serious care and sympa-

---

21. Pelikan, "Personal Memoir," 37.
22. Pelikan, "Personal Memoir," 37.
23. Pelikan provided the following examples: "Tertullian, Athanasius's The Incarnation of the Word juxtaposed with Anselm's Cur deus homo, Augustine, Thomas Aquinas, Luther, Schleiermacher, the nineteenth century." Pelikan, "Personal Memoir," 37.
24. Pelikan, "Personal Memoir," 37.
25. Pelikan, "Personal Memoir," 38.
26. Pelikan, "Personal Memoir," 38.
27. Pelikan, "Personal Memoir," 39–40.

Retrieval for the Sake of Renewal

thetically represented the different views and the variety of key figures in Christian history.

Pelikan reflected on his personal commitment to historic Christian beliefs in comparison to that of his colleagues in the academy. He said, "I was quite out of step with many in my generation, especially among theological scholars at universities, in never having had fundamental doubts about the essential rightness of the Christian faith, but having retained a continuing, if often quite unsophisticated, Slavic piety."[28] In 1996 he retired after fifty years of teaching. In 1998 he left the Lutheran Church to become a member of the Eastern Orthodox Church.[29]

Patrick Henry wrote, "No one in the late twentieth century has attempted a more comprehensive address to the problem of Christian tradition than Jaroslav Pelikan."[30] Robert Wilken comments, "More than any other scholar, [Pelikan] gave the history of Christian thought a public face in the United States."[31]

Pelikan viewed his greatest accomplishments as those that were contributions to Christian churches and theological learning. He reflected, "The two highest recognitions I have ever received for my scholarship were both humanistic rather than theological or ecclesiastical."[32] He said, "But I have been deeply gratified that my historical scholarship has been of service to the Church, its laity as well as its clergy, and to theological seminaries and church colleges across the denominational spectrum, and increasingly, through many translations (including, now, at long last, even translations into Slavic languages), across the globe."[33]

Robert Wilken acknowledges the central place of the church in the career and legacy of Pelikan. He explains, "Though Jaroslav Pelikan had a distinguished career in the university, he was a graduate of Concordia Seminary in St. Louis, where he taught for several years. He always felt at home in a theological community and saw himself, and was revered by others, first and foremost as a *doctor ecclesiae*, a teacher of the Church."[34]

---

28. Pelikan, "Personal Memoir," 32.
29. Pelikan, "Personal Memoir," 32. See also Wilken, "Jaroslav Pelikan," 93–103.
30. Henry, *Schools of Thought*, 1.
31. Wilken, "Jaroslav Pelikan, Doctor *Ecclesiae*," 19–21.
32. The Jefferson Award of the National Endowment for the Humanities in 1983, and the John W. Kluge Prize for Lifetime Achievement in the Human Sciences in 2004.
33. Pelikan, "Personal Memoir," 41.
34. Wilken, "Jaroslav Pelikan, Doctor *Ecclesiae*," 19–21.

Major Contributions from Jaroslav Pelikan

Methodology of Historical Theology

Historical Theology

Jaroslav Pelikan's work *Historical Theology* is "aimed at justifying the historical method of 'doing theology.'"[35] Pelikan said, "It is meant to state some of the principle reasons for the intimate connection between the discipline of history and the study of theology."[36] He explained the aim of the work is "to spell out the methodological assumptions that have guided me in my historical-theological scholarship."[37] Pelikan's definition of historical theology was "the genetic study of Christian faith and doctrine."[38]

Pelikan argued that the quality of the historian's craft provided the integrity of the discipline of historical theology. He claimed that the essential trait of historical theology as a discipline is that it must be "good history."[39] He viewed the importance of historical method as a "matter of acute sensitivity for any historian."[40] He insisted that when the subject of the historical investigation is "Christian doctrine, he [the historian] must intensify that sensitivity."[41] He went on to warn how "in the selection and arrangement of his sources he runs the danger of imposing his theological preconceptions, whether personal or confessional, upon the material."[42]

Pelikan appreciated the intersection between history and theology. He valued both the historical and theological task in the discipline of historical theology. He wrote, "Church history is always more than the history of doctrine, but it should not be less. The historian of doctrine must continue to do his own homework, but he must do it as a historian."[43] Pelikan spoke about the unavoidable theological task in the historical investigation of doctrine:

---

35. Pelikan, *Historical Theology*, ix.
36. Pelikan, *Historical Theology*, ix.
37. Pelikan, *Historical Theology*, ix.
38. Pelikan, *Historical Theology*, xiii.
39. Pelikan, *Historical Theology*, 129.
40. Pelikan, *Historical Theology*, xxii.
41. Pelikan, *Historical Theology*, xxii.
42. Pelikan, *Historical Theology*, xxii.
43. Pelikan, "Essay on the Development of Doctrine," 11.

"He will, of course, find the theological questions in the history of doctrine ineluctable; and in this sense he, too, will have to speak as a theologian."[44]

Pelikan understood the theologian as historian and the historian as theologian. He explained the sense in which the work of the theologian is necessarily linked to history: "Every Christian theologian is, by definition, a historian, for he is charged with responsibility for (and to) a message that has been given and received in the history of the people of God."[45] Likewise, he also argued, "The converse is also true: the historian of the church must be a theologian, and *a fortiori* the historian of Christian doctrine must have a theological ear if he is to interpret the development of the faith and thought of the church with historical integrity and scholarly fidelity."[46] Pelikan believed that the historical task was "a way of making theology meaningful and keeping it honest."[47]

Pelikan believed that theology and history were complementary in the discipline of historical theology. He emphasized the importance of historical integrity for theological effectiveness. He argued that "the more faithful it [historical theology] is to its historical vocation, the more useful it will be in its theological function."[48] He also viewed himself as a theologian.[49] He said, "Theological relevance and methodological clarity may well be among the things that will be 'added unto us' if we seek first the integrity of historical scholarship. This is, finally, what historical theology is about."[50]

Pelikan argued for integrity in historical scholarship: "Exploitation of the history of doctrine for apologetic and evangelistic purposes, even if it were by some chance to be effective, is an injustice to the nature of the sources and to their cultural setting; they deserve to be read historically whether or not they are evaluated theologically."[51]

Pelikan said, "If it is to be the task of historical theology to study the history of Christian doctrine as what has been believed, taught and

---

44. Pelikan, "Essay on the Development of Doctrine," 11.
45. Pelikan, "Tradition, Reformation, and Development," 101–7.
46. Pelikan, "Tradition, Reformation, and Development," 101–7.
47. Pelikan, "Preface," xi.
48. Pelikan, *Historical Theology*, 130.
49. Pelikan referred to himself as "a theologian who stands committed to the faith of orthodox Christendom." See "Theology without God," 671. He also identified as "a Protestant theologian and churchman" in "Catholics in America," 15.
50. Pelikan, *Historical Theology*, xxiii.
51. Pelikan, *Historical Theology*, 80–81.

Delighted by Doctrine

confessed by the church, the enterprise will be beset by historiographical problems of more than ordinary intricacy."[52] Rather than address general issues in historiography, Pelikan chose to "concentrate only on those historiographical issues that confront the historical theologian with a particular urgency."[53] Pelikan concludes that the "soundest historical method to begin with *a posteriori* with that which the Church confesses, *viz*, with dogma."[54]

Pelikan viewed all the historical methods used in historical theology as depending "in part for their procedure upend a recognition of the context of doctrine."[55] He quoted Anders Nygren in support of the principle that understanding doctrines or creeds requires context because what "an idea, belief, or sentiment really means, can only be decided in the light of its own natural context."[56]

David Steinmetz praised Pelikan's skill as a historian saying that he was "a master of his craft."[57] Steinmetz further explained, "He met the past on its own terms, learning the languages, customs, and intellectual assumptions of Christians who inhabited a world very different from his own."[58] Steinmetz also commended Pelikan's writing ability: "He wrote what he learned in a lucid and elegant prose easily accessible to general readers, whatever their worldview."[59] In sum, Pelikan worked diligently as an expert historian to understand his subject and clearly express that understanding to others in a compelling way.

The Vindication of Tradition

In 1983 Jaroslav Pelikan received the Jefferson Award of the National Endowments of Humanities, and he delivered the Jefferson Lectures in the Humanities. These lectures were published in his 1984 work *The Vindication of Tradition*.[60] Mark DeVine comments, "In his little book *The Vindication of Tradition*, Jaroslav Pelikan offers the most compelling case for

---

52. Pelikan, *Historical Theology*, 99.
53. Pelikan, *Historical Theology*, 99.
54. Pelikan, *Historical Theology*, 109.
55. Pelikan, *Historical Theology*, 110.
56. Pelikan, *Historical Theology*, 110. See Nygren, *Agape and Eros*, 35.
57. Steinmetz, "Wide-Angle Historian," 33.
58. Steinmetz, "Wide-Angle Historian," 33.
59. Steinmetz, "Wide-Angle Historian," 33.
60. Pelikan, *Vindication of Tradition*.

Retrieval for the Sake of Renewal

and exploration of the power and the significance of tradition as such and of Christian tradition in particular."[61] The work received a critical review from Bradford E. Hinze[62] and a positive review from Mark Noll.[63]

Ecumenical Historiography

Jaroslav Pelikan's work should be understood as ecumenical historiography. For example, his book *The Riddle of Roman Catholicism* "aims at an interpretation of Roman Catholicism that is sympathetic and critical."[64] Pelikan explained that this book "unites two of the deepest concerns of my thought and scholarship, the Reformation of the sixteenth century and the ecumenical movement of the twentieth."[65]

Pelikan believed, "Lutheranism is ecumenical to the core."[66] He remembered that as a student he came "under the influence of various intellectual and ecclesiastical trends like the ecumenical movement."[67] George took note. He observed, "Pelikan always had a great interest in ecumenical affairs. His book *The Riddle of Roman Catholicism* (1959), written on the eve of the Second Vatican Council, offered an irenic introduction to the world's largest Christian community."[68]

Major Works in Historical Theology

The Christian Tradition

Jaroslav Pelikan contributed major works in historical theology, such as his five-volume work *The Christian Tradition*. Mark Noll notes Pelikan's accomplishment: "Jaroslav Pelikan has written a history of the Christian tradition on a scale no one else has attempted in the twentieth century."[69] First, Pelikan considered this work the culmination of his extensive

---

61. DeVine, "Unacknowledged Heritage," 198.
62. Hinze, Review of *Vindication of Tradition*, 109.
63. Noll, Review of *Vindication of Tradition*, 44.
64. Pelikan, *Riddle of Roman Catholicism*, 13.
65. Pelikan, *Obedient Rebels*, 9.
66. Pelikan, "Form and Tradition in Worship," 23.
67. Pelikan, "Christian Tradition," 29.
68. George, "Delighted by Doctrine," 43–45.
69. Noll, "Doctrine Doctor," para. 1.

teaching career. He said, "Most of my teaching over the years flowed into the project."[70] Second, he viewed this task as his life's work and his calling. He thought of this project "as a special vocation."[71] Lastly, he said his aim was "to write for my generation a successor to Adolf von Harnack's three-volume *Lehrbuch der Dogmengeschichte*."[72] There had not been an attempt to do so. Pelikan lamented, "Therefore, the preparation of a comprehensive history of Christian doctrine had in effect skipped a generation on both sides of the Atlantic."[73]

Timothy George comments, "Pelikan's *magnum opus* eventually became five volumes that he called simply *The Christian Tradition*."[74] George appreciates how Pelikan's historical work captured both the diversity and unity of Christian teaching. He comments on the diverse representation within the volumes, saying, "Pelikan fully recognized the great diversity and varied expressions of Christian teaching across the ages."[75] He recognized a larger thematic unity in Pelikan's writings: "He also stressed the underlying unity and continuity of what the New Testament calls 'the faith that was once for all delivered to the saints' (Jude 3)."[76] Thus, Pelikan as a historian investigated these differences and as a theologian traced the continuity.

In contrast to Harnack, Pelikan said, "I interpreted the formulation of church doctrine as the process by which what was already believed in worship was spelled out in creed and confession. And a major component of my narrative was an examination of the key passages of Holy Scripture that the church claimed to be bringing together in articulating its doctrines."[77] Pelikan traced the origin of doctrine to the expression of believers in the worshipping community based on the authority of biblical exegesis. Jack Forstman wrote, "Without doubt, he is technically as well equipped as anyone since Harnack and probably better equipped than anyone in this generation to give to the [history of doctrine] a new landmark."[78] Forstman said,

---

70. Pelikan, "Personal Memoir," 38.
71. Pelikan, "Personal Memoir," 38.
72. Pelikan, "Personal Memoir," 38.
73. Pelikan, "Personal Memoir," 39.
74. George, "Delighted by Doctrine," 204.
75. George, "Delighted by Doctrine," 204.
76. George, "Delighted by Doctrine," 204.
77. Pelikan, "Personal Memoir," 42.
78. Forstman, Review of *The Christian Tradition*, 96–97.

Retrieval for the Sake of Renewal

"It is doubtful that there is anyone more learned in the history of Christian doctrine or more able to handle his learning with virtuosity than Pelikan."[79]

Timothy George recommends Pelikan's volume on the Reformation as one of his top five classics of Reformation studies. As a specialist in Reformation studies, he commends "the third volume in Pelikan's five-volume set, *The Christian Tradition*."[80] George observed the purpose of each work's cover:

> The cover of each of these volumes is marked by a distinctive color: red for the early church (symbolizing martyrdom), gold for Eastern Christendom (glory), purple for the Latin West (suffering), and sky blue for modernity (the sky is the limit?). The Reformation volume in this series is green—signifying renewal, new life, new beginnings. The chronological parameters place the Reformation in the context of late medieval and early modern times.[81]

George concludes by offering an assessment on Pelikan's work as a whole: "Like nearly everything Pelikan wrote, this is a work of magisterial extent and nuanced detail. Historical theology at its best."[82]

The Christian Creeds

Jaroslav Pelikan completed the four-volume work *Creeds and Confessions of Faith in the Christian Tradition*.[83] In the same way that Pelikan's work on doctrine was intended as a replacement and response to Adolf von Harnack, these volumes can be understood as an update to Phillip Schaff's *The Creeds of Christendom*. The work *Credo: Historical and Theological Guide to Creeds and Confessions of Faith in the Christian Tradition*[84] is a companion and introduction to the three volumes of creeds and confessions compiled by Pelikan and Valerie Hotchkiss.

Robert Wilken comments about the volume: "It should be said that amidst all the historical detail and theological exposition Pelikan has

---

79. Forstman, Review of *The Christian Tradition*, 96–97.
80. George, "My Top Five Classics," para. 5.
81. George, "My Top Five Classics," para. 5.
82. George, "My Top Five Classics," para. 5.
83. Pelikan, *Creeds and Confessions*.
84. Pelikan, *Credo*.

written a vigorous defense of the durability of creedal Christianity."[85] Timothy George describes Pelikan's work on Creeds: "As a capstone to his lifelong interest in the central texts of the Christian faith, Pelikan edited (with Valerie Hotchkiss) what could only be called a second *magnum opus—Creeds and Confessions of Faith in the Christian Tradition*."[86]

The Meaning of Christian Doctrine

Jaroslav Pelikan defined Christian doctrine: "What the church of Jesus Christ believes, teaches, and confesses on the basis of the word of God: this is Christian doctrine."[87] In the fourth volume of his works, he referred to this definition of Christian doctrine eight times.[88] This repetition is pointed out in a review of the first volume by Robert Calhoun[89] as well as a review of the second volume by Carl Peter.[90] Eileen Serene reviewed the third volume: "In this rendition medieval theology emerges as less polemical and less abstract than we have come to assume. Much of this difference in impression is due to Pelikan's clearly stated working definition of theology as 'what the church believed, taught, and confessed on the basis of the Word of God.'"[91] Peter wrote about the second volume of *Christian Tradition*: "This volume repeats the definition of Christian doctrine given in the first and refers to it regularly."[92] Pelikan viewed his statement of Christian doctrine as a historical description of the subject, not as a theological prescription as such: "All this is, strictly speaking, a description rather than a definition of Christian doctrine."[93]

Pelikan claimed, "The historian of the church must be a theologian, and *a fortiori* the historian of Christian doctrine must have a theological ear if he is to interpret the development of the faith and thought of the church with historical integrity and scholarly fidelity."[94]

85. Wilken, "Credo," 39.
86. George, "Delighted by Doctrine," 44.
87. Pelikan, *Christian Tradition*, vol. 1.
88. Pelikan, *Christian Tradition*, 4:6, 8, 127–28, 134–35, 217, 306, 341, 352.
89. Calhoun, Review of *The Christian Tradition*, 501.
90. Peter, Review of *The Christian Tradition*, 313.
91. Serene, Review of *The Christian Tradition*, 489–90.
92. Peter, Review of *The Christian Tradition*, 313.
93. Pelikan, *Christian Tradition*, vol. 1.
94. Pelikan, "Tradition, Reformation, and Development," 101.

Retrieval for the Sake of Renewal

Reception and Transmission by Timothy George

Timothy George offers a description of his study of Christian history and makes a prescription for those interested in studying Christian history: "I never had Jaroslav Pelikan as a classroom teacher, but I was one of his students, as everyone seriously interested in Christian history has to be."[95] First, he *describes* his personal study by saying, "I was one of his students."[96] Second, he *prescribes* what ought to be the case for other students of Christian history. He says about becoming a student of Pelikan: "as everyone seriously interested in Christian history has to be."[97] George is a student of Pelikan through his writings and considers him his intellectual mentor: "As a young student of historical theology, I once determined to read everything Pelikan had written."[98] He considers Pelikan the "best church historian America has ever produced."[99]

George dedicated his work *Evangelicals and Nicene Faith* with these words: "Sacred to the memory of Jaroslav Pelikan 1923–2006."[100] In the introduction to this work George establishes, "Jaroslav Pelikan has defined Christian doctrine as 'what the church of Jesus Christ believes, teaches, and confesses on the basis of the Word of God.'"[101]

George writes of Pelikan, "the deepest passion of his soul—to tell the story of the Christian tradition in all of its fullness, drama, coherence, romance, and rigor, thereby exposing the deepest textures of meaning inherent in the Christian message itself."[102]

Dogma beyond Anathema

In 1987 George quotes Pelikan at the beginning of his faculty address at the Southern Baptist Theological Seminary: "Historical theology is the genetic study of Christian faith and doctrine. It is, to quote Jaroslav Pelikan,

---

95. George, "Delighted by Doctrine," 205.
96. George, "Delighted by Doctrine," 205.
97. George, "Delighted by Doctrine," 205.
98. George, "Delighted by Doctrine," 205. See Hotchkiss for a recent list of Pelikan's works, "Bibliography of Jaroslav Pelikan," 185–231.
99. George, "Delighted by Doctrine," 205.
100. George, *Evangelicals and Nicene Faith*, v.
101. Pelikan, *Christian Tradition*, vol. 1.
102. George, "Delighted by Doctrine," 43.

Delighted by Doctrine

who quotes the Formula of Concord, the study of what the church of Jesus Christ 'believes, teaches, and confesses as it prays and suffers, serves and obeys, celebrates and awaits the coming of the Kingdom of God.'"[103] He makes an *implicit* reference and *explicit* quotation from Pelikan. The implicit reference is when George says, "Historical theology is the genetic study of Christian faith and doctrine."[104] He borrows this definition of historical theology directly from Pelikan.[105]

Theology of the Reformers

Timothy George writes in the preface to *Theology of the Reformers*, "The noted Elizabethan scholar, A. L. Rowse, once complained that 'the sixteenth century is full of the useless fooleries of disputes about doctrine.'"[106] He then frames his entire work using Pelikan's definition of Christian doctrine: "This book is essentially about such disputes, and it assumes that they were neither useless nor foolish insofar as they form a significant chapter in the history of what the church of Jesus Christ 'has believed, taught and confessed on the basis of the Word of God.'"[107]

In the introduction of *Theology of the Reformers*, George also states, "Historical theology is the study of what 'the church of Jesus Christ believes, confesses, and teaches on the basis of the Word of God.'"[108] He adds, "The church of Jesus Christ, however, is universal in respect to time as well as space. The reformers we study are both our fathers in the faith and our brothers in the community of the faithful. Their struggles and doubts, their victories and defeats are also ours."[109] He comments, "Jaroslav Pelikan once wrote about 'the tragic necessity of the Reformation.'"[110]

---

103. George, "Dogma beyond Anathema," 701. See Pelikan, *Development of Christian Doctrine*, 143. See Schaff, Article 1 of the Formula of Concord in *Creeds of Christendom*, 3:93–94.

104. George, "Dogma beyond Anathema," 701.

105. Pelikan, *Historical Theology*, xiii.

106. Rowse, quoted in George, *Theology of the Reformers*, 5. See Pelikan, *Christian Tradition*, vol. 1.

107. George, *Theology of the Reformers*, 5. See Pelikan, *Christian Tradition*, vol. 1.

108. George, *Theology of the Reformers*, 20. George quotes Pelikan, *Christian Tradition*, vol. 1.

109. George, *Theology of the Reformers*, 20.

110. George, *Theology of the Reformers*, 2.

Retrieval for the Sake of Renewal

Are Baptists a Creedal People?

Timothy George categorizes the slogan, "No creed but the Bible," as a part of the Campbellite movement in the nineteenth century.[111] He laments that it "has become axiomatic in many circles as a marker of Baptist identity today."[112] George offers a different approach to creeds based on the Baptist tradition by pointing out that "prior to the twentieth century, most Baptist theologians, from Andrew Fuller to E. Y. Mullins, spoke very affirmingly of 'the Baptist creed.'"[113] He says that Baptist theologians "strongly rejected the idea that voluntary, conscientious adherence to an explicit doctrinal standard was somehow foreign to the Baptist tradition."[114]

George clarifies that the Baptist tradition has been cautious in two important ways regarding the authority and use of creeds. He explains the first caution is based on the priority of religious liberty: "First, Baptists of all theological persuasions have been ardent supporters of religious liberty, opposing sometimes to the point of persecution, imprisonment, and all kinds of degradations, state-imposed religious conformity, and the attendant civil sanctions associated therewith."[115] The priority of religious liberty is based on their faith-commitment that "God alone is the Lord of the conscience."[116] The implication was "Baptists deny that civil magistrates have any legitimate authority to regulate or coerce the internal religious life of voluntary associations, including churches."[117] Therefore, on the basis of religious liberty, creeds should not be used in such a way that they are imposed on the conscience of people by their civil authorities.

George explains that the second caution is based on the priority of biblical authority. He claims that Baptists have "never agreed that any humanly constructed doctrinal statement should be elevated to a par with

---

111. George, "Is Jesus a Baptist?," 94–95. Dockery and George comment, "Sometimes the phrase 'no creed but the Bible' is just a shibboleth for neither creed nor the Bible." Dockery and George, *Great Tradition of Christian Thinking*, 68.

112. George, "Is Jesus a Baptist?," 94–95.

113. George, "Is Jesus a Baptist?," 94–95.

114. George, "Is Jesus a Baptist?," 94–95. See George, introduction to *Baptist Confessions, Covenants, and Catechisms*, 3. George comments, "The idea that voluntary, conscientious adherence to an explicit doctrinal standard is somehow foreign to the Baptist tradition is a peculiar notion not borne out by careful examination of our own heritage."

115. George, "Is Jesus a Baptist?," 94–95.

116. George, "Is Jesus a Baptist?," 94–95.

117. George, "Is Jesus a Baptist?," 94–95.

Holy Scripture, much less placed above it."[118] He gives an example of how Baptist confessions relate to the biblical authority. He says, "The confessions themselves invariably declare, the Bible alone remains the *norma normans* for all teaching and instruction, 'the supreme standard by which all human conduct, creeds, and religious opinions should be tried.'"[119]

George contrasts the historic Baptist approach with the approaches of Eastern Orthodoxy and Roman Catholicism. First, he points out how Eastern Orthodoxy "elevates the conciliar decisions of the first seven ecumenical councils to an infallible status."[120] Second, he observes how Roman Catholicism "does the same thing with all twenty-three ecumenical councils, as they count them (including Vatican II)."[121] Lastly, he comments, "Baptists have never 'canonized' any of their confessions. Rather, we have held them all to be revisable in the light of the Bible, God's infallible, unchanging revelation."[122]

George claims that creeds and confessions should focus on primary doctrines. He believes that when the church loses focus on primary doctrines the result is that the mission of the church is compromised. He argues that a lack of theological perspective is present "when matters of secondary and tertiary importance are elevated to a level of primary significance and are placed right next to the doctrine of the Trinity or justification by faith."[123] George illustrates this concern by quoting Pelikan that tradition is "defined as the living faith of the dead, to traditionalism, which is the dead faith of the living."[124] He warns against traditionalism: "Retrieval can lead to reversal as well as to renewal."[125]

George comments on the use of *The Baptist Faith and Message* in the Southern Baptist Convention: "If the Baptist Faith and Message becomes a grab bag for every problem or issue that arises, then it will cease to be a consensual statement of Baptist conviction."[126] George believes that S. M.

---

118. George, "Is Jesus a Baptist?," 94–95.
119. George, "Is Jesus a Baptist?," 94–95.
120. George, "Is Jesus a Baptist?," 94–95.
121. George, "Is Jesus a Baptist?," 94–95.
122. George, "Is Jesus a Baptist?," 94–95.
123. George, "Is Jesus a Baptist?," 94–95.
124. George, "Is Jesus a Baptist?," 94–95.
125. George, "Is Jesus a Baptist?," 94–95.
126. George, "Is Jesus a Baptist?," 94–95.

Retrieval for the Sake of Renewal

Noel has "words of wisdom for us here."[127] Noel said that Baptist doctrinal standards "should be large enough to meet the exigencies of the church by preserving her while in the wilderness, exposed to trials, in peace, purity, and loyalty. And it should be small enough to find a lodgment in the heart of the weakest lamb, sound in the faith."[128]

Despite these concerns with creeds, biblical authority, and religious freedom, George applauds the value and use of creeds: "Evangelicals today are finding that the historic creeds of the church are a resource for faith and spiritual life. Evangelicals are engaged in a process of retrieval for the sake of renewal. In this way, they are coming to stand side by side with Orthodox and Catholic believers in affirming the Nicene faith of the early church."[129] George then quotes Pelikan to clarify what he means by the faith that creeds defend: "Jaroslav Pelikan has defined Christian doctrine as 'what the church of Jesus Christ believes, teaches, and confesses on the basis of the Word of God.'"[130]

A Life Fit for Eternity

On December 15, 2018, Timothy George gave the commencement address to the graduates of Samford University before his retirement in 2019.[131] George charged the students with a quotation from Goethe taken from Jaroslav Pelikan's *The Melody of Theology: A Philosophical Dictionary*. Goethe said, "What you have received as heritage, take now as task, and thus you will make it your own."[132] In *Evangelicals and Nicene Faith* George refers to how "Pelikan loved to quote this line from Goethe, his favorite poet."[133]

Conclusion

Jaroslav Pelikan made significant contributions to Timothy George's understanding of historical theology through his definition of Christian doctrine

---

127. George, "Is Jesus a Baptist?," 94–95.
128. Quoted in George, "Is Jesus a Baptist?," 95.
129. George, *Evangelicals and Nicene Faith*, v.
130. George, *Evangelicals and Nicene Faith*, v. See Pelikan, *Christian Tradition*, vol. 1.
131. George, "Life Fit for Eternity."
132. Goethe quoted in Pelikan, *Melody of Theology*, 102.
133. George, "Delighted by Doctrine," 203.

as well as offering his methodology for and significant works in historical theology. This chapter offered a brief sketch of Pelikan's teaching career and scholarship, and it identified the major contributions that influenced George's approach to historical theology.

George carried on the contributions of Pelikan in his work as a historical theologian in the study of Christian doctrine and the use of Christian creeds. George looked to Pelikan as a model of a historical theologian, in his definition of Christian doctrine, his methodology, and his major works. The central question of this book, Timothy George's understanding of historical theology, has been established in terms of significance (chapter 1); biographical context (chapter 2); the first key influencer, George Huntston Williams (chapter 3); the second key influencer, David Steinmetz (chapter 4); and chapter 5 has examined the last of the three key influencers, Jaroslav Pelikan.

Contributions from Jaroslav Pelikan in the study of Christian doctrine (chapter 5) provided additional components of Timothy George's understanding of historical theology. Chapter 6 will explain how George brings together the influences of Williams, Steinmetz, and Pelikan in his understanding of the "hierarchy of ecclesial identity." It will also consider the implications of his understanding of historical theology for the academic theologian and pastor theologian.

6

Evangelical Ecumenism
Timothy George's Understanding of Historical Theology

> I am a Trinitarian Christian who by the grace of God belongs to the whole company of the redeemed through the ages.
>
> —TIMOTHY GEORGE

Introduction

THE CENTRAL QUESTION OF this book focuses on Timothy George's understanding of historical theology. George's approach has been established in terms of significance (chapter 1) and biographical context (chapter 2). His first key influencer, George Huntston Williams, made major contributions to George's understanding of historical theology such as church history as a theological discipline, social activism, and ecumenism (chapter 3). His second key influencer, David Steinmetz, made major contributions to George's understanding of historical theology such as historiography and the history of biblical interpretation (chapter 4). His last key influencer, Jaroslav Pelikan, made major contributions to George's understanding of historical theology such as methodology of historical theology, major works in historical theology, and the meaning of Christian doctrine (chapter 5).

Evangelical Ecumenism

Chapter 6 explores the essence and implications of Timothy George's understanding of historical theology.

How does George, a Baptist preacher from Chattanooga, Tennessee, appreciate and assimilate the various influences on his work, such as the Harvard scholar George Huntston Williams (who was a Unitarian), the Duke scholar David Steinmetz (who was a Methodist), and the Yale scholar Jaroslav Pelikan (who was a Lutheran and later Eastern Orthodox)? George's proposal, which he calls a hierarchy of ecclesial identity, reveals how he views himself and how he relates to other Christians.

The four *notae ecclesiae* found in the *Nicene Creed* best summarize George's understanding of historical theology. These words are also known as the four marks of the church. The *Nicene Creed* confesses belief "in one, holy, catholic, and apostolic Church."[1] These four marks characterize his approach to historical theology, and they are necessary for the discipline to be of benefit to the church.

The Hierarchy of Ecclesial Identity

Timothy George's proposal, known as the "hierarchy of ecclesial identity,"[2] is the key to understanding his approach to historical theology, as well as making sense of the diverse influences of Williams, Steinmetz, and Pelikan. He views himself as "a Protestant, an evangelical, and a Baptist."[3] Nevertheless, he does not accept any of these descriptions as his "spiritual and ecclesial identity at the most basic core level."[4] While he does not minimize these traits, he does not see them as his central identity.

George acknowledges that these ecclesial traits are "important markers of my place within the community of faith."[5] He reveals, "There is a more primary identity I must confess: I am a Trinitarian Christian who by the grace of God belongs to the whole company of the redeemed through the ages, those who are 'very members incorporate in the mystical body' of Christ (*Book of Common Prayer*)."[6] He sees himself as more than a member

---

1. Berardino, *We Believe in One*, 1.
2. George, "Why I Am an Evangelical," 94.
3. George, "Why I Am an Evangelical," 94.
4. George, "Why I Am an Evangelical," 94.
5. George, "Why I Am an Evangelical," 94.
6. George, "Why I Am an Evangelical," 94.

of his denomination in his time; he sees himself as a member of the whole body of Christ throughout all time.

George's proposal of a hierarchy of ecclesial identity as a pattern of thought builds on an approach to levels of doctrine which he learned from Catholic theologians, who refer to a "hierarchy of truths."[7] Vatican II's *Decree on Ecumenism* includes this concept.[8] George clarifies what Catholic theologians mean by their concept.

George comments that a "hierarchy of truths" does not imply "that some truths are truer than others or that the Catholic faithful are free to pick and choose among the teachings of their church as they please."[9] He writes, "It means, rather, that in the economy of divine revelation, more theological weight, as it were, is given to those teachings that relate directly to the foundational truths of the Christian faith."[10] The truths that are *in accordance* with foundational truths carry more weight, while the truths that are only *in relation* to foundational truths carry less weight.

Christian Identity

Timothy George uses the martyrdom story of Polycarp to illustrate the central importance of Christian identity rather than other secondary labels or loyalties. He writes, "When Polycarp of Smyrna, a disciple of the apostle John, was brought before the Roman tribunal before being cast into the arena with wild beasts, he confessed publicly the faith that he knew would lead to his certain martyrdom."[11] The Christian identification with the person and work of Jesus Christ is a spiritual identity worth dying for both in the first and the twenty-first centuries.

George imagines what the possible labels could have been, which Polycarp could have self-associated, and ultimately he points to Polycarp's confession to make his claim about the centrality of Christian identity.

---

7. George, "Is Jesus a Baptist?," para. 1.

8. Flannery, *Unitatis Redintegratio*, 11.

9. George, "Is Jesus a Baptist?," para. 1.

10. George, "Is Jesus a Baptist?," para. 1. For a recent evangelical use of a hierarchical approach to theological truths see Ortlund, *Finding the Right Hills*. George also points out how Aquinas, in a similar way, distinguishes between articles of faith that are *secundum se* and others *in ordine ad alia*. Thomas Aquinas, *Summa Theologica Volume II: Part II-II*, q.1, a.6. George recommends "the excellent study by the Capuchin scholar William Henn." See "Hierarchy of Truths," 439–71.

11. George, "Why I Am an Evangelical," 94.

Evangelical Ecumenism

George says, "In that critical moment, Polycarp did not say, 'I am a Paulinist. I am a Petrist. I am an Ignatian' (after his great contemporary Ignatius of Antioch). Nor did he say, 'I am an Irenaean' (after his famous disciple, Irenaeus of Lyon). Rather he confessed, 'Christianus sum' ('I am a Christian')."[12] George offers Polycarp's confession of Christian identity amidst the severe persecution of the early church as an example to contemporary Christians today to challenge them to make their priority commitment to Christ above all other labels.

George's commitment to Christ is above all labels, not without any labels. He warns, "Yet the desire for a Christianity shorn of all particularity carries its own risks."[13] He gives examples of how this has already been attempted in biblical and historical accounts and failed.

George begins with a biblical example: "The Corinthian church of the New Testament had its own 'factious titles': the Paul-party, the Peter-sect, the Apollos-coterie."[14] He explains how these divisions resulted in frustration, and "another group in the church at Corinth arose claiming to have no mere human leader at all: 'We belong to Christ,' they said."[15] This alternative did not prove to be an adequate solution because "the Christ-party at Corinth was soon beset by the same spirit of arrogance and divisiveness that marked all the other partisan groups in the congregation."[16] This example in the New Testament demonstrates that ecclesial identity should not enable arrogance and divisiveness. Solely claiming Christ does not exempt someone from the same pitfalls.

George selects an example from history that is representative of "a recurring theme throughout the history of the church."[17] He refers to the attempt by Alexander Campbell in the nineteenth century, who tried "to eliminate denominational labels and restore the one true Christian church."[18] Campbell's attempt failed.[19] George explains, "Within a single generation, his movement had subdivided into several distinct and often

---

12. George, "Why I Am an Evangelical," 94.
13. George, "Is Jesus a Baptist?," para. 4.
14. George, "Is Jesus a Baptist?," para. 4.
15. George, "Is Jesus a Baptist?," para. 4.
16. George, "Is Jesus a Baptist?," para. 4.
17. George, "Is Jesus a Baptist?," para. 4.
18. George, "Is Jesus a Baptist?," para. 4.
19. For an evaluation of Alexander Campbell's movement and engagement with the Baptist tradition see George, "Southern Baptist Ghosts," 18–24.

mutually hostile church bodies."[20] He says that Campbell's failure should not surprise "anyone familiar with the history of Presbyterians in Scotland, Lutherans in America, Reformed churches in the Netherlands, Anglicans in Africa, and Baptists almost anywhere."[21]

Evangelical Identity

In 1999 Timothy George wrote the article "If I'm an Evangelical, What Am I?"[22] George argues that Evangelicals "lay claim to the doctrinal legacy of the Reformation, the missionary and evangelistic impulse of the Great Awakening, and a trans-denominational fellowship of Bible-believing Christians with whom we share a common commitment to the Word of God and the task of world evangelization."[23] George defines evangelicalism as "a renewal movement within historic Christian orthodoxy."[24] Therefore, "it cannot be equated with any one denomination."[25] Instead, he views evangelicalism by its theological commitments.[26]

The first theological commitment is the "trinitarian and christological consensus of the early church."[27] The second theological commitment is "the formal and material principles of the Reformation."[28] The third theological commitment is "the missionary movement that grew out of the Great Awakening."[29] The fourth theological commitment is "the new stirrings of the Spirit that indicate 'surprising works of God' are still happening in the world today."[30]

George links evangelicals within Christian orthodoxy and in line with it: "Evangelicals stand in continuity with the Great Tradition of Christian

---

20. George, "Is Jesus a Baptist?," para. 4.
21. George, "Is Jesus a Baptist?," para. 4.
22. George, "If I'm an Evangelical, What Am I?"
23. George and Dockery, *Theologians of the Baptist Tradition*, 7.
24. George, "Is Jesus a Baptist?," para. 5.
25. George, "Is Jesus a Baptist?," para. 5.
26. See Packer and Oden, *One Faith*, 19–20. Packer and Oden also use a theological approach to defining evangelicalism. For a recent historical examination of evangelicalism see Kidd, *Who Is an Evangelical?*.
27. George, "Is Jesus a Baptist?," para. 5.
28. George, "Is Jesus a Baptist?," para. 5.
29. George, "Is Jesus a Baptist?," para. 5.
30. George, "Is Jesus a Baptist?," para. 5.

believing, confessing, worshiping and acting through the centuries, while not discounting the many local histories that must be written to give a full account of Christian communities in any given era."[31]

Baptist Identity

Timothy George's Baptist identity began when he came to know Christ: "I am a Baptist because it was through the witness of a small Baptist church that I first heard the gospel of Jesus Christ."[32] He also grew in his spiritual journey through the ministry of his Baptist church: "Many of the things I still believe in I first learned in that modest Baptist community of faith."[33] Thus, he came to know Christ through a Baptist church and he continued to grow as a Christian in a Baptist church.

George's Baptist identity was not only inherited, through his early conversion and formation, but also was chosen through careful reflection and study. He reflects, "I came to see that being a Baptist was for me the most faithful way of being an evangelical, a Protestant, and a Christian."[34] It was when he "studied the Bible more deeply"[35] and "became aware of many other church traditions, doctrines, and denominations"[36] that his "Baptist convictions grew stronger."[37]

Just as George views his evangelical commitments as the best way to be a faithful Christian, he also sees his Baptist commitments as the best way to be an evangelical. He reasons, "If evangelicalism at its best is a renewal movement within the one holy, catholic, and apostolic church, then the Baptist

---

31. George, "Is Jesus a Baptist?," para. 5.

32. George, "Why I Am an Evangelical," 108.

33. George, "Why I Am an Evangelical," 108. George mentions the doctrine of Christology and atonement. He says, "Jesus loves me and died on the cross for my sins." He formed a strong conviction about the Bible during this time: "The Bible is the totally true and trustworthy Word of God." He had a basic anthropology "that all human beings are made in the image of God and are infinitely precious in his sight." His calling to the ministry: "When I was called to preach the gospel, it was in a Baptist church that I was set apart and ordained as a minister of the divine Word."

34. George, "Why I Am an Evangelical," 108.

35. George, "Why I Am an Evangelical," 108.

36. George, "Why I Am an Evangelical," 108.

37. George, "Why I Am an Evangelical," 108.

Retrieval for the Sake of Renewal

tradition represents a renewal within the renewal."[38] He places his Baptist tradition within evangelicalism, which is within historic Christianity.[39]

George claims that Baptists share a common commitment to Christian orthodoxy. He summarizes:

> With all true Christians, Baptists profess loyalty to Jesus Christ the Lord, the eternal Son of the heavenly Father who 'For us and our salvation' became man. He died for our sins on a cross, rose triumphantly over death, ascended to the Father, and one day will come again in power and glory. In the meantime, he still reigns, rules, and redeems through the Holy Spirit.[40]

George calls on Baptists to recover their historic Christian commitments: "All Baptists need to cultivate a holistic orthodoxy, based on a high view of the Scriptures and congruent with the trinitarian and Christological consensus of the early church."[41] He claims that there is no other way to "avoid the dangers of rigid reductionism on the one hand and liberal revisionism on the other."[42]

George describes the Baptist movement in terms of its continuity and differences.[43] First, he establishes the continuity of Baptists with the Reformers and Evangelicals: "The Baptist tradition finds a place within this narrative as a distinctive reform movement within the wider evangelical renewal, a reform within the reform, so to say."[44] Second, he distinguishes Baptists from other evangelical groups of the Reformation: "Baptists are indeed heirs of the Reformation, but they are not, nor have they ever been, mere clones of Luther, Calvin, Zwingli, the Anabaptists,

---

38. George, "Why I Am an Evangelical," 102.

39. George and Dockery, "Future of Baptist Theology," 5. George positions the Baptist tradition in line with historical Christianity: "Baptists are orthodox Christians who stand in continuity with the dogmatic consensus of the early church on matters such as the scope of Holy Scripture (canon), the doctrine of God (Trinity), and the person and work of Jesus Christ (Christology)."

40. George, "Is Jesus a Baptist?," para. 6.

41. George and Dockery, *Theologians of the Baptist Tradition*, 6.

42. George and Dockery, *Theologians of the Baptist Tradition*, 6.

43. For a "good overview of Baptist history" George recommends resources for a general understanding of Baptist history: Bebbington, *Baptists through the Centuries*; Chute et al., *Baptist Story*; McBeth, *Baptist Heritage*. See George, "Baptist Theologian: Reflections on Anglicanism," 233.

44. George, "Is Jesus a Baptist?," para. 6.

or anyone else."⁴⁵ Thus, Baptists are in continuation with the Reformation, yet maintain a unique and distinct ecclesial identity from the other groups of the Reformation.

George addresses the distinct formation and unique contribution of the Baptist tradition. The context of Baptist beginnings was characterized by "persecution and dissent."⁴⁶ He explains, "Baptists began as a small, persecuted minority in pre-revolutionary England."⁴⁷ A unique contribution of Baptists was an "intense advocacy of religious freedom and, especially in the American setting, the separation of church and state (which does not equal the divorce of religion from public life)."⁴⁸

George admits that while he is grateful to be a Baptist, his denominational affiliation has not been without its challenges: "Being a Baptist is a blessing but also sometimes a burden. From time to time I have considered the possibility of becoming something else."⁴⁹ For example, he remembers, "I once prepared a talk called 'The Confessions of a Catholic-Friendly, Pentecostal-Admiring, Reformed Baptist with a Hankering after Lutheranism and a Strong Affinity for the *Book of Common Prayer*.'"⁵⁰

George explains how he is able to benefit from other traditions while maintaining his Baptist identity:

> Each of these ecclesial traditions, among others, has enriched my life and calling to serve the Body of Christ. Each brings distinctive treasures to our common labors *pro Christo et ecclesia*. Being a Baptist gives me all the freedom I need to appropriate as fully as I can the gifts they offer without abandoning the Baptist principles and ways that I cherish.⁵¹

The Essence of Timothy George's Historical Theology

Timothy George's understanding of historical theology begins with George Huntston Williams and his notion of "church history as a theological

---

45. George, "Is Jesus a Baptist?," para. 6.
46. George, "Is Jesus a Baptist?," para. 6.
47. George, "Foreword," to *Baptists and the Christian Tradition*, 1.
48. George, "Foreword," to *Baptists and the Christian Tradition*, 1.
49. George, "Is Jesus a Baptist?," para. 10.
50. George, "Why I Am an Evangelical," 109.
51. George, "Is Jesus a Baptist?," para. 13.

discipline." It is from Williams and then Pelikan that George embraces ecumenism. George defines church history as "the attempt to recall and recount the story of the people of God, in all of its manifold variations and to do so from the perspective of someone who recognizes that retelling, that reinvestigation, as his or her own story, which is to say from the perspective of faith."[52] Thus, he claims, "This is why church history is not just secular history with a little sanctimonious water of baptism thrown over it."[53]

Historiography

George grounds his approach in the nature and function of history. He relates human perspective to the study of history: "Any sense of history grows out of the fact that we perceive ourselves and the world around us in terms of our finitude. We are finite beings limited in two respects: by space and by time."[54] He addresses the limitation of space: "The fact that you were born in a certain place, in a particular culture, within a specific family is going to a very great extent affect the kind of person that you become. We are spatial beings."[55] He also comments on the limitation of time: "But also the fact that you were born on a certain day, within a given decade or century or millennium is also going to place inescapable parameters around you and the kind of person you become."[56] Therefore, humans are historical creatures.

George argues that the purpose of studying history, of ransacking the past, is "to enlarge one's coordinates to move away from that particular intersection of time and space in which we find ourselves and to gain perspective on our self and culture."[57]

George sets his approach to historical theology in contrast with the view of Harvey Cox, specifically the idea known as the "principle of genealogical selectivity." Cox argued:

> As late twentieth-century Christians trying to work out a viable spirituality, there are two principal historical sources to which we should look. They are the earliest period of our history and the most recent, the first Christian generations and the generation just

---

52. George, "Church History as a Theological Discipline."
53. George, "Church History as a Theological Discipline."
54. George, "Church History as a Theological Discipline."
55. George, "Church History as a Theological Discipline."
56. George, "Church History as a Theological Discipline."
57. George, "Church History as a Theological Discipline."

before us... the ransacking of other periods for help in working out a contemporary spirituality soon becomes either antiquarian or downright misleading.[58]

George responds, "Cox's counsel against 'ransacking' the past reflects an attitude common in American culture in general, especially within evangelicalism. It reflects what might be called the heresy of contemporaneity or, in less theological terms, the imperialism of the present."[59] He explains, "What do I mean by this term? In the Middle Ages, everyone believed that the earth was at the center of reality, that the whole created cosmos was ordered in relation to what we now know, thanks to Copernicus, is a mere speck of dust among myriads of constellations and galaxies."[60]

George suggests, "The Copernican revolution was a paradigm shift. It radically altered our view of space. But we have yet to experience a similar revolution with respect to time."[61] He laments, "We still place ourselves, our values, our worldview at the center of history, relegating whole epochs to the Dark Ages or pre-Enlightenment culture."[62] He warns, "Thus the Christian past, including ways earlier generations of believers have understood the Bible, becomes not so much something to be studied and appropriated as something to be ignored or overcome."[63]

Ecclesiology

Timothy George's ecclesiology has a diachronic emphasis: "The church is the Body of Christ extended throughout time as well as space. It encompasses all of the redeemed of all of the ages. This is a reality already glimpsed in the New Testament by the writer of Hebrews who admonished the believers in his day."[64] Thus, George emphasizes the universal nature of the church.

George defines the church in both universal and local terms. First, he addresses the local nature of the church: "Now, what is the church?

---

58. Cox, *Turning East*, 157.
59. George, *Reading Scripture with the Reformers*, 23.
60. George, *Reading Scripture with the Reformers*, 23.
61. George, *Reading Scripture with the Reformers*, 23.
62. George, *Reading Scripture with the Reformers*, 23.
63. George, *Reading Scripture with the Reformers*, 23.
64. George, "Is Jesus a Baptist?," para. 7.

The church is local, it is congregational, it is particular, it is covenantal."[65] Second, he asserts the universal nature of the church: "Yes, but the church in the NT is also universal, it is ecumenical; it is the one, holy, catholic, and apostolic church. As the Baptist Faith and Message says, 'The church is the company of all the redeemed of all the ages.'"[66] He affirms the church as both local and universal: "Thus the church has both a local and a universal dimension, both a congregational and an associational form, both a covenantal and an ecumenical thrust, always and ever grounded on our confession in the one God who is forever Father, Son, and Holy Spirit."[67]

George's area of research and specialty, his "interest in the Reformation was always in service to a wider concern, namely, to understand the reformers as they saw themselves: faithful servants of Jesus Christ in the one, holy, catholic, and apostolic church."[68] David Dockery agrees, "The Nicene Creed, an important fourth-century confession, describes the church as one, holy, catholic or universal, and apostolic."[69] Dockery also sees these traits as marks of Christians who "are called to exemplify love and truth, oneness and holiness, catholicity and apostolicity."[70] Thus, these marks epitomize George's approach to historical theology.[71]

George carries on the charge of his mentor, George Huntston Williams: "The two parts of the creed that the church historian is to make meaningful are *Una Sancta*, the one, holy, catholic, and apostolic church; and *Communio Sanctorum*, the church as the communion of saints."[72]

Oneness: An Ecumenism of Conviction

The scope of historical theology should be the *one* church, rather than a single denomination or sect. In other words, historical theology should be ecumenical historiography at its best. Timothy George's commitment to

---

65. George, "Faith, My Faith," 89.

66. George, "Faith, My Faith," 89. See Southern Baptist Convention, "2000 Baptist Faith and Message."

67. George, "Faith, My Faith," 89.

68. Wax, "Theology of the Reformers."

69. Dockery, "Foreword," 12.

70. Dockery, "Foreword," 12.

71. See also George, "What I'd Like to Tell."

72. George, "Remembering George Huntston Williams," 10:48–11:03.

Evangelical Ecumenism

this type of ecumenism began with his mentor George Huntston Williams (chapter 3) and was modeled by Jaroslav Pelikan (chapter 5).

George clarifies his approach to ecumenism: "I believe in an ecumenism of conviction, not an ecumenism of accommodation. We do not advance the cause of Christian unity by abandoning our biblical understanding of the church. But how do we hold these together?"[73] In light of this tension between conviction and unity, George offers three ways to move forward.

First, Christians should "recognize the centrality of Jesus Christ. The closer we come to Jesus Christ, the closer we come to one another as brothers and sisters in him."[74] Second, Christians should study the Bible together. George explains, "The Bible belongs to the whole people of God, not just to one denomination or church tradition. We can clarify differences and find a deeper unity by going deeper into the Scriptures."[75] Third, Christians should pray together. George writes, "Jesus prayed to his heavenly Father (John 17:21) that his disciples would be one so that the world might believe. We can join our prayer to the prayer of Jesus and in so doing become a part of its fulfillment."[76]

George claims that a theologian for *the church* must be a theologian for *the whole church*. He said, "An ecclesial theologian must also be an ecumenical theologian—ecumenical in the sound, orthodox sense of that word."[77] George explains, "That means, a pastor theologian is concerned with the entire people of God through the ages and also with the *missio Dei* throughout the entire *oikoumenc* today, that is, the whole inhabited world (Luke 2:1)."[78]

George clarifies the relationship between the community of faith from which the theologian stands and the wider community of faith. He says, "Such pastors honor and cherish the discrete traditions from which they come, but they also know themselves to belong to the one, holy, catholic, and apostolic church, which is the Body of Christ extended throughout time as well as space."[79] Therefore, he argues, "Theology that is truly biblical

---

73. Berry and Hottman, "Baptists and Ecumenism," 90.
74. Berry and Hottman, "Baptists and Ecumenism," 90.
75. Berry and Hottman, "Baptists and Ecumenism," 90.
76. Berry and Hottman, "Baptists and Ecumenism," 90.
77. George, "Foreword," to *The Pastor Theologian*, 8.
78. George, "Foreword," to *The Pastor Theologian*, 8.
79. George, "Foreword," to *The Pastor Theologian*, 8.

and evangelical is done for, with, and in the context of this enlarged Ecclesia for which Christ died."[80]

George uses the metaphor of gift exchange to best understand the relationship between his particular community of faith and the wider community of faith: "Baptists have special gifts to offer the wider Body of Christ and also lots to learn from our fellow Christians. At Beeson, you can do both at once with grace, goodwill and gospel hospitality."[81]

Holiness: Retrieval for the Sake of Renewal

The goal of historical theology should be the progressive *holiness* of the church. Historical theology contributes to the holiness of the church through its project of retrieval for the sake of renewal, thus seeking to rescue the church from its amnesia.[82] Timothy George carries on David Steinmetz's quest (Chapter 4) to free the church from amnesia. The continuing influence of Steinmetz and George is evident in the work of Michael Allen and Scott Swain in the *New Studies in Dogmatics* series. Allen and Swain aim to construct theology "in a program of renewal through retrieval."[83] The goal of pursuing theology is achieved by "drawing more deeply upon the resources of Holy Scripture in conversation with the church's most trusted teachers (ancient, medieval, and modern) who have sought to fathom Christ's unsearchable riches."[84]

George diagnoses the spiritual problems facing the church today: "The two major diseases of the contemporary church are spiritual amnesia (we have forgotten who we are) and ecclesiastical myopia (whoever we are, we are glad we are not like 'them'). While these maladies are not unique to the people of God called Baptists, they are perhaps most glaringly present among us."[85]

George recalls when his love for teaching church history and theology began while at Southern: "I found that students knew little, if anything, about those pioneers of the past, and I wanted to encourage a program of *ressourcement*—not a return to 'the good old days' but an appropriation of

---

80. George, "Foreword," to *The Pastor Theologian*, 8.
81. George, *Baptists at Beeson*, 5.
82. George, "Remembering David Steinmetz's Quest."
83. Allen and Swain, "Introduction to New Studies."
84. Allen and Swain, "Introduction to New Studies."
85. George and Dockery, *Theologians of the Baptist Tradition*, 1.

the warranted wisdom and spiritual insight they can offer to the church today."[86] George's purpose of recalling the history of God's people is renewing the holiness of God's people in the present.

Catholicity: Christian Doctrine

The context of historical theology should be an expression of *catholicity* by learning from the grand scope of the Christian tradition. This has been best exemplified by the five-volume work *The Christian Tradition* by Jaroslav Pelikan (chapter 5). There have been recent discussions within different denominations on how each can best pursue catholicity, such as Baptists in *Baptists and the Christian Tradition* (2020),[87] as well as Presbyterians in *Reformed Catholicity* (2015).[88] Mark Dever observes that church catholicity "came to be used synonymously with 'orthodox.'"[89]

George defines the church as "the body of Christ extended throughout time as well as space. It encompasses all of the redeemed of all of the ages."[90] C. S. Lewis compared the Church catholic as a hall and church traditions as rooms. He illustrated the Church catholic as "a hall out of which doors open into several rooms. If I can bring anyone into that hall I shall have done what I attempted."[91] Lewis compared specific church traditions as rooms: "But it is in the rooms, not in the hall, that there are fires and chairs and meals. The hall is the place to wait in, a place from which to try the various doors, not a place to live in."[92] This illustration from Lewis captures George's affirmation of both the catholic or universal Church and Church denominations.

George commends the "reclaiming of Baptist tradition, especially its catholicity, seen in the writings and work of a number of younger theologians."[93] He highlights the work of "the Center for Baptist Renewal, whose principal participants identify as Southern Baptists."[94] He has

---

86. George, "*SBJT* Forum," 111.
87. Emerson et al., *Baptists and the Christian Tradition.*
88. Allen and Swain, *Reformed Catholicity.*
89. Dever, *Church*, 18. See also Dever, "Catholic Church," 71–72.
90. George, "Why I Am an Evangelical," 107.
91. Lewis, "Preface," xv.
92. Lewis, "Preface," xv.
93. George, "Baptist Theologian," 231.
94. George, "Baptist Theologian," 231.

promoted the goals of the center by writing an article for *First Things*[95] and interviewing Luke Stamps on the *Beeson* podcast.[96]

Apostolicity: Biblical Exegesis

Historical theology is not a distraction from, but an aid to, the church's *apostolicity*. The historical theologian should share a commitment to understand the content of the Apostolic teaching in God's word by engaging with the long exegetical tradition of the church. Timothy George carries on the work of David Steinmetz, who helped scholars "see the interpretive tradition of the church not as a problem to be overcome, but rather as an indispensable aid for rightly understanding the inspired Word."[97] George contributes to the church's understanding of the exegetical tradition through his work *Reading Scripture with the Reformers* and through his role as the general editor of the *Reformation Commentary Series*.

George defines apostolicity in Protestant and Baptist terms. He explains, "Baptists do not define apostolicity in terms of a literal lineal succession of duly ordained bishops who alone have authority to ordain other ministers. Instead, Baptists define apostolicity in terms of the primordial character of the gospel, the inscripturated witness of the apostles, and the succession of apostolic proclamation."[98]

George believes that contemporary Christians should read Scripture in community with "the fathers, the scholastics and the reformers."[99] He observes, however, a "dialectic of primitivism or presentism establishes two centers of scriptural engagement—the first Christian generation, which means the writings of the New Testament, and the most recent generations, notably my generation."[100] He warns, "This dichotomy governs the way Scripture is read in much of the Christian community today, both in liberal mainline churches and in conservative evangelical ones. There is, we might say, a presentist imperialism of the left and a presentist imperialism of the right."[101]

95. George, "Retrieval for the Sake of Renewal."
96. George, "Baptist Renewal."
97. George, "Remembering David Steinmetz's Quest." See Steinmetz, "Superiority of Pre-Critical Exegesis," 27–38.
98. George, "Baptist Theologian," 242.
99. George, *Reading Scripture with the Reformers*, 23.
100. George, *Reading Scripture with the Reformers*, 23.
101. George, *Reading Scripture with the Reformers*, 23.

The Implications of Timothy George's Historical Theology

Seminary Curriculum

To borrow imagery from C. S. Lewis's *The Lion, The Witch and the Wardrobe*, Timothy George's perspective of historical theology is the wardrobe that seminary students can walk through to get to Narnia, an exciting new place where they discover the wonderful works of Augustine, Aquinas, Calvin, Luther, Wesley, and many others.

George writes, "At Beeson we practice an ecumenism of conviction, not an ecumenism of accommodation."[102] George explains the unique ecumenical seminary environment of Beeson Divinity School: "Our charter documents call for us to be Christian, Protestant, evangelical, and interdenominational. We also like the words 'catholic,' 'orthodox,' 'Reformational,' and 'ecumenical.' Beeson is a place where Baptists and Anglicans alike, along with believers from many other denominations, have been able to find *koinōnia* in our core commitment to Jesus Christ and in our love for his body, the church—the one, holy, catholic, and apostolic church."[103]

George revised the theological curriculum based on his perspective of historical theology and the needs of the evangelical and interdenominational context of Beeson Divinity School. When referring to systematic theology and church history, he claims, "We've abolished them."[104] He clarifies, "That is to say, we no longer have two stack poles and try to relate them disjunctively, but we brought them together in a sequence we call history and doctrine."[105] He describes the sequence of history and doctrine saying, "The effort is to look chronologically, but in a more systematic doctrinal way at the movement in the history of God's people of how these ideas have arisen and how they shape Christian life."[106]

George's approach to Christian theology, built on his interpretation of Williams, Steinmetz, and Pelikan, has become known at Beeson Divinity School as "history and doctrine."[107] George's perspective on historical

---

102. George, "Baptist Theologian: Reflections," 228.
103. George, "Baptist Theologian: Reflections," 227.
104. George, "Conversation on Theology," 20:12–14.
105. George, "Conversation on Theology," 20:14–23.
106. George, "Conversation on Theology," 20:24–35.
107. See "Historical and Doctrinal Studies," esp. the "Program Design" section. "Unique in theological education, Beeson teaches theology and church history together in an integrated four-course sequence. Students learn key doctrines such as Scripture,

theology is the missing piece to the puzzle of how to train and teach students in the evangelical and interdenominational context of Beeson Divinity School.

George reveals how his understanding of historical theology influenced the theological curriculum of Beeson Divinity School, as well as informed all of his writing ministry:

> Several years ago at Beeson Divinity School we undertook a major revision of our curriculum, bringing together church history and systematic theology into an organic whole, a new integrated discipline that we call History and Doctrine. This approach has shaped everything I have written, including *Theology of the Reformers*. There is no such thing as a disembodied theology divorced from the mess and muck of real life. This is clearly stated in the central affirmation of the Christian faith: 'The Word became flesh and dwelt among us' (John 1:14).[108]

George elevates the place of historical theology in theological schools. He claims, "Church history is the most important subject in the theological curriculum."[109] He asserts, "I say this not only because I am a church historian but simply because it is true."[110] He explains, "Without a good grasp of the history of God's people through the ages one cannot understand the Bible, doctrine, ethics, ecumenism, spiritual formation or any other topic related to the life of faith."[111] He argues that historical theology provides the necessary perspective, background, and formation for all the other fields of study.

Ministry Leadership

Timothy George believes that historical theology is "a theological discipline rooted in the self-revelation of the biblical God, the God who makes and keeps covenant with his people."[112] Therefore, George regards historical theology as "enormously relevant to the task of proclamation, the primary

---

Christology, Pneumatology, justification, creation, and anthropology as they unfold and develop in the history of the Christian church."

108. Wax, "Reformation Theology or Theologies?," para. 5.
109. George, "Evangelical Reflection on Scripture," 191.
110. George, "Evangelical Reflection on Scripture," 191.
111. George, "Evangelical Reflection on Scripture," 191.
112. George, "*SBJT* Forum," 89.

Evangelical Ecumenism

job of every God-called minister of the gospel."[113] George concludes, "I dare to say that, apart from the direct study of the Holy Scriptures themselves, no discipline in the theological curriculum is more important for the sermon preparation of the preacher."[114]

George begins with the importance of the history of exegesis for the ministry leader. He encourages the preacher: "We do not come to the study of the Bible alone but in the company of the whole people of God, the body of Christ scattered throughout time as well as space."[115] Thus, historical theology offers the history of exegesis as an indispensable resource in the preacher's study.

George challenges the preacher to not fall into the pitfalls of primitivism or presentism: "It is not sufficient for the preacher to have the New Testament in one hand and the latest word from Bultmann, Käsemann, or Conzelmann, or even the current evangelical gurus, in the other."[116] Therefore, the preacher must embrace the history of exegesis or else go the way of Harvey Cox by way of either a fundamentalist reduction or liberal revision.

The theological basis of George's reasoning is pneumatological: "The Holy Spirit did not abandon the Church with the death of the apostles, and we have much to learn as we 'read alongside' the church fathers, schoolman reformers, and theologians of ages past."[117] The spiritual gift of teaching God's Word in the present and the past has the same source, the Holy Spirit. The ministry leader should benefit from the Holy Spirit's illumining work among God's people as they study the Bible throughout church history.

George recognizes the limitations of the history of exegesis: "None of their interpretations is inerrant, and we must subject them all to the divine touchstone of God's perfect revelation in the Bible—*sola scriptura!*"[118] Thus, he reinforces the ultimate authority of Scripture and the importance of engaging the history of exegesis and evaluating the claims of past interpretation in light of sound biblical interpretation.

George considers the role of church history in writing his commentary on Galatians.[119] He remembers, "In writing my commentary on Ga-

---

113. George, "*SBJT* Forum," 89.
114. George, "*SBJT* Forum," 89.
115. George, "*SBJT* Forum," 89.
116. George, "*SBJT* Forum," 89.
117. George, "*SBJT* Forum," 89.
118. George, "*SBJT* Forum," 90.
119. George, *New American Commentary: Galatians*.

latians for the *New American Commentary Series*, I gained much insight from Tertullian, Chrysostom, Augustine, Aquinas, Luther, Calvin, William Perkins, John Brown, and many others."[120] These voices from the past contain insight and wisdom for today.

George also recommends the value of sermons from the past: "In addition to studying commentaries and exegetical works, it is also good to see how a particular text has been preached in different historical moments. The sermons of Spurgeon, Wesley, and Knox are a rich treasury."[121] Thus, the preacher can discern not only what the text meant to the original audience, but what the text has meant throughout history.[122]

George points out how the development of doctrine equips the ministry leader: "The discipline of symbology, that is, the study of confessions, creeds, and catechisms, reveals the ebb and flow of doctrinal understanding throughout the history of the church. God has frequently used the occasion of heresy to bring orthodoxy to full clarity."[123] Therefore, the ministry leader does not need to re-invent the wheel with every doctrine every time he or she faces a difficult theological question.

George raises the question: "Why do we need these humanly constructed statements of faith, the creeds and confessions of the church, to proclaim the faith, once for all entrusted, passed on?"[124] He answers this question by referring to when his family lived for a year in Switzerland, especially taking note of the dangerous curves driving through the Alps.[125]

George remembers relying on the guardrails while driving through the Alps.[126] He compares the purpose of the development of doctrine with the necessity of guardrails: "Our confessions of faith are like those guardrails."[127] He starts by addressing the danger involved, "When you are traveling dangerous mountain roads, you are glad someone has put those guardrails in place."[128]

---

120. George, "*SBJT* Forum," 90.
121. George, "*SBJT* Forum," 90.
122. George, "Dogma beyond Anathema," 701.
123. George, "*SBJT* Forum," 90.
124. George, "Faith, My Faith," 84.
125. George, "Faith, My Faith," 84.
126. George, "Faith, My Faith," 84.
127. George, "Faith, My Faith," 84.
128. George, "Faith, My Faith," 84.

George distinguishes between the guardrails and the road in the same way he distinguishes between the development of doctrine and the biblical revelation of Jesus Christ. He explains, "Now you do not want to confuse the guardrails with the road and start driving up there on the guardrails—then danger is really imminent! Stay on the road. The road is Jesus Christ. He said: 'I am the Way (the Road), the Truth and the Life' (John 14:6)."[129] In the same way that the guardrails support but are secondary to the road, the development of doctrine supports but is secondary to the biblical revelation of Jesus Christ.

George concludes why the church needs these guardrails to stay faithful to God's Word: "But we need guardrails as we are tempted this way and that in the history of the church, guardrails to keep us on the road guided by the light that is the Holy Scriptures: 'Thy Word is a lamp unto my feet, and a light unto my path' (Ps 119:105 KJV)."[130] Thus, he maintains the primacy of Scripture and the centrality of Jesus Christ while urging the use of necessary secondary sources.

George offers the doctrine of the Trinity and the doctrine of grace as examples for which the ministry leader must appreciate their historical development: "How can anyone preaching on the doctrine of the Trinity ignore the great struggle between Arius and Athanasius in the fourth century? Likewise, in studying the doctrines of grace, we are theologically bereft if we know nothing of the debate between Augustine and Pelagius, or between Luther and Erasmus."[131]

George clarifies what he means: "This does not mean that every sermon must be filled with historical allusions to these doctrinal developments. But every sermon should be informed by them as we seek in our own day to pass on the faith intact to the next generation."[132]

George offers that church history can serve the preaching ministry of the local church as a valuable resource for illustration and application. He explains, "Doctrinal preaching has both a propositional and incarnational dimension. It is the truth of God's word distilled and applied to fallen and redeemed human beings, but it is also that truth lived out in the flesh and

---

129. George, "Faith, My Faith," 84.
130. George, "Faith, My Faith," 84–85.
131. George, "Faith, My Faith," 84–85.
132. George, "*SBJT* Forum," 89.

Retrieval for the Sake of Renewal

blood reality of the people of God."[133] Church history provides many examples of the truth lived out.

George presents the Christian past as a source of lived theology, a shared human experience through which listeners can relate and find inspiration. Church history is not abstract or impersonal. He explains, "In an era when narrative preaching and personal autobiographical reminiscence has become the norm in many pulpits, I think we should extend the scope of our narrative reach to include those who are now, by God's grace, in the Church Triumphant."[134] He claims, "Our lives and our stories are intertwined with theirs, and we have much to learn about living the Christian life today from a close acquaintance with their failures and faithfulness, their suffering and perseverance."[135] While he is honest about the failures of Christians in the past, he maintains there is still much to learn from their lives.

George believes that many of the disagreements in the church concerning worship reveal a "near-total ignorance of historical precedence and liturgical developments."[136] He suggests the way to remedy this is by connecting "great hymns of the faith with sound biblical and theological exposition."[137] He provides the following examples:

> Who could not preach on the grace of God after singing Charles Wesley's "And Can It Be"? Or, on forgiveness after "Praise, My Soul, The King of Heaven"? Likewise, in celebrating the ordinances of baptism and the Lord's Supper, the "visible words" of God in bread, cup, and water should always be accompanied by thorough instruction.[138]

He concludes, "In these and many other ways, church history is a wonderful resource for the preaching ministry of the Church."[139]

---

133. George, "*SBJT* Forum," 89.
134. George, "*SBJT* Forum," 91.
135. George, "*SBJT* Forum," 91.
136. George, "*SBJT* Forum," 89.
137. George, "*SBJT* Forum," 89.
138. George, "*SBJT* Forum," 89.
139. George, "*SBJT* Forum," 89.

Evangelical Ecumenism

Conclusion

The central question of this book, Timothy George's understanding of historical theology, has been established in terms of significance (chapter 1); biographical context (chapter 2); his first key influencer, George Huntston Williams (chapter 3); his second key influencer, David Steinmetz (chapter 4); and his last key influencer, Jaroslav Pelikan (chapter 5).

George's approach to historical theology emphasizes the theological value of church history, or in his words, "church history as a theological discipline."[140] The four marks of ecclesiology summarize George's approach to historical theology. He looks to the church in space and time to learn from its oneness (the unity of the church), holiness (the renewal of the church), catholicity (the whole tradition), and apostolicity (the basis of Scripture).

Chapter 6 has explained how George brings together the influences of Williams, Steinmetz, and Pelikan through his proposal of a hierarchy of ecclesial identity. George, as a historical theologian, commits to the four marks of the church through his emphasis on Christian unity, spiritual formation, Christian doctrine, and biblical exegesis. The implications of his understanding of historical theology for the academic theologian and the pastor theologian demonstrated the relevance for theological schools and local churches.

Final Conclusion

Central Question

This book has argued that Timothy George's understanding of historical theology is an interpretation of George Huntston Williams, David Steinmetz, and Jaroslav Pelikan. Therefore, this present study employed the method of intellectual biography to explore how these three personal influences shaped George's historical and theological approach.

This work studied George's approach by placing him in the context of the professors that formed his perspective. George Huntston Williams modeled ecumenism, social activism, and church history as a theological discipline. David Steinmetz detailed historiography and biblical interpretation. Jaroslav Pelikan modeled the method of historical theology, major works in historical theology, and the meaning of Christian doctrine. This

---

140. George, "Church History as a Theological Discipline."

book argued that all three of these influences combine to inform George's intellectual approach to historical theology in his teaching, scholarship, and leadership.

This book addressed the central question of Timothy George's understanding of historical theology in terms of its significance (chapter 1), biographical context (chapter 2), conceptual formation (chapter 3–5), and definition (chapter 6). Chapters 3–5 answered who are the key influencers that shaped George's understanding of historical theology and revealed how he defines Christian doctrine and its historical orientation and development. Chapter 6 addressed the characteristics that define George's approach to historical theology.

Research Summary

Chapter 1, "Introduction," addressed why Timothy George and his view of historical theology are worthy subjects of this book. This chapter established the significance of George's understanding of historical theology by surveying his widespread influence and work. This book offers the first book-length analysis of George's understanding of historical theology by describing and analyzing the key figures that shaped him. This work is the first study of the thought of Timothy George as an interpretation of George Huntston Williams, David Steinmetz, and Jaroslav Pelikan. George has written more than twenty books and has served in both theological education and local church ministry; however, this is the first book devoted to George's approach to historical theology.

Chapter 2, "Hell's Half Acre, Harvard, and Historical Theology: Timothy George (1950–)," presented an overview of George's early life, his Harvard Divinity School education, his teaching career at Southern Seminary, and the accomplishments of his work at Beeson Divinity School of Samford University in Birmingham, Alabama. This chapter presented relevant background information which provided a personal context for understanding Timothy George. This chapter identified and reflected on key developmental scenes and experiences in George's formative years. This chapter provided the background for how he came to be influenced by three key figures: George Huntston Williams, David Steinmetz, and Jaroslav Pelikan.

Chapter 3, "A Holy Calling, to Keep Truth Alive: George Huntston Williams (1914–2000)" began the focus on George Huntston Williams's influence on George's perspective of historical theology. What are the components that make up Timothy George's understanding of historical theology? Who are the key persons and events that shaped George's understanding of Christian doctrine and the purpose of historical theology? This chapter addressed those questions by presenting a profile of George Huntston Williams. The profile examined his major contributions: church history as a theological discipline, ecumenism, and social activism. These contributions influenced George's approach to historical theology in terms of his calling and work as a historical theologian in the following areas: History and Doctrine, Evangelicals and Catholics Together (ECT), and the *Manhattan Declaration*.

Chapter 4, "The Quest to Free the Church from Amnesia: David Steinmetz (1936–2015)" presented a profile of David Steinmetz and demonstrated his influence on George's understanding of historical theology. The profile examined Steinmetz's major contributions to George's understanding of historical theology through his writings in the historiography of historical theology as well as offering the foundation for and multiple works in the history of biblical interpretation. This chapter offered a brief sketch of Steinmetz's teaching career and scholarship, and it identified the major contributions that influenced George's approach to historical theology. George carried on the contributions of Steinmetz in his work as a historical theologian in the areas of Reformation studies and the history of biblical exegesis. George looked to Steinmetz as an example of a committed churchman, a beloved teacher, and a scholar.[141]

Chapter 5, "Delighted by Doctrine: Jaroslav Pelikan (1923–2006)," presented a profile of Jaroslav Pelikan and demonstrated his influence on Timothy George's understanding of historical theology. Pelikan made significant contributions to George's understanding of historical theology through his definition of Christian doctrine as well as his methodology for and significant works in historical theology. This chapter offered a brief sketch of Pelikan's teaching career and scholarship, and it identified the major contributions that influenced George's approach to historical theology. George carried on the contributions of Pelikan in his work as a historical theologian in the study of Christian doctrine and the use of Christian creeds. George looked to Pelikan as the model historical theologian in terms of his definition of Christian doctrine, his methodology, and his major works.

---

141. George, "Remembering David Steinmetz's Quest."

Retrieval for the Sake of Renewal

Chapter 6, "Evangelical Ecumenism: Timothy George's Understanding of Historical Theology," brought together the influences of Williams, Steinmetz, and Pelikan, and explored George's view of and work in historical theology. This chapter presented George's understanding of the "hierarchy of ecclesial identity" by examining his identity as a Christian, Baptist, and evangelical. His ecclesial identity is the foundation for developing a unique approach to historical theology. This chapter argued that the essence of George's historical theology is found in the traits of ecclesiology: oneness (ecumenism), holiness (renewal), catholicity (Christian doctrine), and apostolicity (biblical exegesis). These traits provide principles for practicing historical theology for the church with Timothy George as a model for the academic theologian.

George's views and practice of historical theology have ministry implications for the pastor theologian. This chapter also considered changes to current models of theological education curriculum by arguing for the inclusion, integration, and prioritization of historical theology in the theological curriculum. This chapter outlined implications for the academic theologian and the pastor theologian and brought the book to a close by offering key findings from George's view of historical theology through a summary of the main arguments presented throughout the book.

Further Research

This research aimed to provide a strong framework and pathway for further studies of Timothy George, Christian doctrine, and the task of historical theology. First, the life and ministry of Timothy George deserve a book-length biographical account. In light of the work of institutional history, Beeson Divinity School at Samford University is now thirty-four years old and, since George retired, is now led by its second dean Douglas Sweeney. This transition calls for an extensive and careful institutional history of Beeson Divinity School and the leadership of its first dean.

Second, interdenominational schools, such as Beeson Divinity School, and ecumenical theologians, like Timothy George, raise questions concerning how to maintain denominational identity while learning from and working with Christians from other denominations on theological matters and social concerns.

Third, the development and historical context of Christian doctrine deserves greater recognition in the seminary curriculum. More should be considered, researched, and evaluated in light of the theological value of church history and its place within contemporary theological education as well as its relationship to other fields of study.

Fourth, the task of historical theology, its method, its scope, and its purpose should be further researched by a closer examination of each of the premier historical theologians explored in this book: Timothy George, George Huntston Williams, David Steinmetz, and Jaroslav Pelikan. Future historical theologians will do well to retrieve their orthodox theological convictions, genuine spiritual depth, and careful historical-theological method.

Afterword

A Reflection by Timothy George

I RECALL VERY WELL the day Christopher Hanna stopped by my office for a visit. I knew Chris both as a recent graduate of Beeson Divinity School, scholarly and bright, and as a strategic leader in the ministry of a dynamic local church. People come to the Office of the Dean for all kinds of reasons, and I had no idea what Chris had on his mind that day. It soon became evident. Chris was about to begin a program of doctoral research and wanted to make my work as a theologian and historian of the church his primary focus. I undertook at once a ministry of discouragement. There were many better objects, I told Chris, on which to hone his considerable scholarly skills. When he persisted, I made a counter suggestion: that his research focus not so much on me but on some of the great teachers and scholars with whom I had been privileged to study. Chris took my advice, and the result is the book you now hold in your hand.

Before I comment on the three scholars identified in this book as major influencers, there is a prior question: how did I become a historian in the first place? As the product of a broken home, I was brought up by two great-aunts, both of whom were wonderful women who loved and encouraged me. But neither could read or write. The wider world of language, culture, and ideas was conveyed to me through two institutions in my hometown of Chattanooga: the public library and the public school. From the first grade on, I was blessed to have access to great books and great teachers. I think of Lillian Patton, who drilled us in Latin; of Lucille Johnson who taught poetry

Afterword

as though she had just come from a conversation with William Blake; and especially of James Duke, my high school baseball coach, who also taught what was called in that long-ago time "world civilization." Coach Duke was a pretty good baseball coach, but he was a fabulous classroom teacher. He made history come alive—scintillating stories, gripping narratives, battles that mattered, and ideas that would not die. Intuitively, Coach Duke knew that it was a mortal sin to make history boring. I have spent my life as a teacher determined not to do so myself.

George Huntston Williams, a Harvard Unitarian who believed in the Holy Trinity; David C. Steinmetz, a Methodist who knew more about Calvin than any Presbyterian or Baptist I have met; Jaroslav Pelikan, a Missouri Synod Lutheran who became Eastern Orthodox—together they modeled to me both the possibility and the necessity of advancing a form of historical theology that was at once confessional and ecumenical, one that was as narrow as Peter's declaration, "You are the Messiah, the Son of the Living God" (Matt 16:16), and as wide as the mission of the church—unto the uttermost parts of the earth. Though they differed from one another in many different ways, they each conveyed to me important principles about what it means to be, in the words of Cotton Mather, one of "the Lord's remembrancers," principles that continue to shape my vocation as a historical theologian in the service of the church.

1. George Huntston Williams and the Church as the Body of Christ through Time as Well as Space

I first encountered George Williams's *magnum opus*, *The Radical Reformation*, when I was an undergraduate majoring in history at the University of Tennessee at Chattanooga. First published in 1962, this book is a massive tome of more than 1500 pages in its third revised edition. Neither before nor since have I read anything so daunting, so intricate, so coherent, so compelling. I remember saying to myself, "Wow, I have to study with the person who wrote this book!" Williams is best known for *The Radical Reformation*, an important book which defined an entire field of study for several generations. At the same time, it occupied only a small part of his remarkable scholarly output. He wrote about liturgical kingship in the Middle Ages, patristic Christology in the early church, Celtic monasticism, American Puritanism, incipient Pentecostalism, requirements for the ministry, and the history of education, including his remarkable three-volume

Afterword

set called *Divinings: The History of Religion at Harvard Over Three Centuries*. For Williams, the church was the body of Christ extended through time as well as space. Both the grandees of church history about whom he wrote, such as Athanasius, Anselm, and Luther, and a host of dissenters, what one critic dubbed "George's ragtag band of radicals"—deserved careful attention because without exception they have something to teach us about the multi-colored wisdom of God (Eph 3:10). No Christian thinker can be a pure Platonist (as Saint Augustine discovered) without lapsing into heresy, just as no Christian thinker can be a strict Aristotelean (as Saint Thomas discovered) without losing the essence of the gospel. Still, most theologians lean one way or the other. I have followed my great teacher George Williams in tilting toward Plato.

2. David C. Steinmetz and the History of the Church as the History of Biblical Exegesis

It was Gerhard Ebeling who first said that church history is nothing other than the history of exegesis, but it was David Steinmetz who forged an entire school of thought along this line. Sometimes a scholarly article or essay can have more impact than a book and such as the case with Steinmetz's groundbreaking, "The Superiority of Pre-Critical Exegesis" (1980). This essay was at once a severe critique of the historical critical study of the Bible in its reductionistic extremes and a positive call for a fresh engagement with the reception of Holy Scripture throughout the history of the church. Steinmetz was an important formulator of what is called today the Theological Interpretation of Scripture. When I was asked to serve as the general editor of the *Reformation Commentary on Scripture*, a twenty-nine-volume set of sixteenth-century biblical comment, David Steinmetz became an original member of our editorial advisory board and remained a formative influence on the project especially through his many students who became volume editors.

David Steinmetz was also flat-out the best classroom teacher I ever had. Students scurried to get to his class on time and were never anxious to leave. I once described what it was like to be a student in Steinmetz's classroom:

> He was simply the best classroom teacher I have ever had. He was not only brilliant, but also passionate and insightful. He never lost sight of the larger context of the texts and traditions he was so adept at bringing to life. I shall never forget his early morning

Afterword

lectures in Andover Hall, as he presented Calvin's life and thought like a great actor commanding the stage. He never took roll; no one dared miss his lively lectures—replete with chalk-drawn diagrams on the blackboard, lively interrogations of the 16th-century texts, and dramatic enactments of Reformation debates. You felt like you were *there* with Luther and Zwingli at Marburg, with Calvin and Bolsec in Geneva.[1]

3. Jaroslav Pelikan and the Reformation as Tragic Necessity

George Williams was a Protestant observer at all four sessions of the Second Vatican Council. There he first met Karol Wojtyła, then a young bishop from Poland, who would become Pope John Paul II. Williams developed a close friendship with the Polish pope and later wrote *The Mind of John Paul II*, the first book about him in English. More than anyone else, Williams inspired my own ecumenical efforts which led to my appointment as a fraternal delegate representing the Baptist World Alliance at the Synod for the New Evangelization in 2012. But Jaroslav Pelikan, a close friend and colleague of Williams, also played a key role in my ecumenical formation. On the eve of the Second Vatican Council, Pelikan published a book called *The Riddle of Roman Catholicism* in which he spoke about the "tragic necessity of the Reformation."[2] The tragic side of the Reformation is seen not only in the deeper rupture of Western Christendom that occurred in the sixteenth century, but in the violence, persecution, and bloody wars of religion that marked that era. But on the other hand, the necessity of the Reformation can also be recognized in many movements of spiritual renewal, in the good news of God's free and unfettered grace which marked the revival of Augustinian theology, and especially in the recovery and renewed study of the Bible which continues to shape all sectors of the church today.

I once suggested that Luther's great maxim *simul iustus et peccator*, can apply not only to individuals but also to particular epochs and episodes in the history of the church. One of Pelikan's wisest statements in this regard relates to the development of doctrine and the continuity between the classical creeds of Christianity and the distinctive concerns of the Protestant Reformation. "If the Holy Trinity was as holy as the Trinitarian dogma

---

1. George, "In Honor of David Steinmetz," para. 3.
2. Pelikan, *Riddle of Roman Catholicism*, 46.

Afterword

taught; if original sin was as virulent as the Augustinian tradition said it was; and if Christ was as necessary as the Christological dogma implied—then the only way to treat justification in a manner faithful to the best of the Catholic tradition was to teach justification by faith."[3] Near the end of his life, Pelikan completed a three-volume set of the *Creeds and Confessions of Faith in the Christian Tradition*. I was greatly honored when he invited me to provide an endorsement for this project. I commended it as "the definitive edition of the primary documents of Christian belief and worship—complete with a masterful interpretation of the meaning of these texts. The remarkable collection will be used for generations to come."

The Heidelberg Catechism is one of my favorite documents of the Reformation. It opens with a ringing declaration of Jesus Christ as "our only comfort in life and death," and centers throughout on the theme of praise and gratitude to God. I am grateful to God for George Huntston Williams, David C. Steinmetz, and Jaroslav Pelikan whose life and witness so illuminated my own calling and work as a theologian in the service of the church. Of course, they are only three among many others on whose shoulders I have sat and in whose tracks I have trod. Someday in heaven, I hope to thank them all with more profundity and a deeper joy than this fleeting life allows. Finally, in the meantime, I want to thank Chris Hanna for bringing this all together with competence and clarity in a book I trust will inspire a new generation of the "Lord's remembrancers."

—Timothy George is distinguished professor at Beeson Divinity School of Samford University and general editor of the twenty-nine-volume *Reformation Commentary on Scripture*.

---

3. Pelikan, *Obedient Rebels*, 47–48.

Appendix 1

Overview of Timothy George's Published Work

THE PRIMARY WORKS BY Timothy George display his thought and illuminate the primary influences that have shaped his understanding of historical theology.

Selected Works by Timothy George: 1980s

In 1982 George wrote *John Robinson and the English Separatist Tradition*, which is the published version of his doctoral dissertation.[1] The preface is of significant interest. George acknowledges Professor William Wright for first awakening his interest in the Reformation. He also acknowledges George Huntston Williams as his mentor and thesis advisor. He comments on the significant influence that Willams had on his theological education.

In 1984 in the article, "Three Marks of the Church," George examines the essential components of a church.[2] Historical theology is done for the benefit of the church and is about the church. Therefore, there must be clarity and definition regarding the church. This article offers insights into George's ecclesiology.

---

1. George, *John Robinson*.
2. George, "Three Marks of the Church," 28–30.

Appendix 1

In 1985 in the article "Systematic Theology at Southern Seminary," he surveys and evaluates the theological instruction of the Boyce Era, the Mullins Era, and the Post-War Era at Southern Seminary.[3] He also comments on the instruction of historical theology during these time periods at the seminary. George held positions in both the department of church history and the department of theology at Southern Seminary.

In 1986 in the article, "A Right Strawy Epistle: Reformation Perspectives on James," George argued that the history of theology is the story of how the church has interpreted the Bible.[4] He references Gerhard Ebeling who argued that the history of theology as well as the history of the Christian church should be understood through its interpretation of the Bible. He offers a case study by focusing on how the Reformers understood and interpreted the book of James.

In 1986 in the article "George Huntston Williams: A Historian for All Seasons," Timothy George examines Williams's distinctive understanding of church history as a theological discipline.[5] The work was originally presented at a session of the American Academy of Religion in New York City in 1982. The presentation was in honor of his mentor George Huntston Williams.

In 1987 in "Dogma Beyond Anathema: Historical Theology in the Service of the Church," George offers a full statement of his perspective of historical theology.[6] This document introduces George's view of historical theology as a discipline and its benefit to the church.

In 1988 he published *Theology of the Reformers*, wherein George examines the theological self-understanding of five Reformation figures.[7] He views the Reformation not merely in terms of political, economic, or social factors. He argues that the Reformation was primarily a religious event and at its core, a theological event. In the introduction he defines the task of historical theology for the reader to understand the book's subject and intent.

In the 1989 article, "The Reformation Roots of the Baptist Tradition," George addresses the relationship between Baptists and the heritage of the Reformation.[8] He offers his views of Baptist origins, distinctives, and beliefs

---

3. George, "Systematic Theology at Southern Seminary," 31–47.
4. George, "Right Strawy Epistle," 369–82.
5. George, "George Huntston Williams," 75–93.
6. George, "Dogma Beyond Anathema," 691–713.
7. George, *Theology of the Reformers*, 14–15.
8. George, "Reformation Roots of the Baptist Tradition," 9–22.

in light of the Reformation. He explores themes in Baptist Theology and examines their Reformation heritage. These themes include the doctrine of God, Christology, Holy Scripture, and ecclesiology.

Selected Works by Timothy George: 1990s

In his 1990 article, "Partly Fearing, Partly Hoping: Evangelicals, Southern Baptists, and the Quest for a New Consensus," George reviews and responds to Carl F. H. Henry's book, *Confessions of a Theologian*.[9] He examines the relationship between Southern Baptists and evangelicalism. He considers the reasons why each of the groups is attracted to one another because of their mutual appreciation while addressing the concerns and barriers for identification and cooperation.

In 1990 in the article "Southern Baptist Relations with Other Protestants," George evaluates the priority of Christian unity and the activity of Southern Baptists.[10] He identifies patterns from the 1880s to 1919, and he addresses key developments from 1919 to 1990. He concludes by considering what type of future relationships Southern Baptists might have with other Protestants.

In 1994 George provides an exposition of Galatians in his work, *The New American Commentary: Volume 30, Galatians*.[11] He reflects on the works of John Calvin and Martin Luther as he exegetes the text of Galatians. He attempts to bring the disciplines of theology and exegesis together. He views his commentary as a "theological exposition."[12]

In 1996 in the article "Why We Still Need Luther," George profiles Martin Luther.[13] He establishes Luther's time and place as well as his key contributions. He explains how Luther's legacy should still inspire and guide the church today.

In 1999 in the article "If I'm an Evangelical, What Am I?" George offers a definition of evangelicalism through the lens of historical theology.[14] He evaluates and critiques David Bebbington's quadrilateral. He defines the Evangelical movement in light of the Great Tradition.

9. George, "Partly Fearing, Partly Hoping," 167–72.
10. George, "Southern Baptist Relations," 24–34.
11. George, *New American Commentary: Galatians*.
12. George, "Preface," 16.
13. George, "Why We Still Need Luther."
14. George, "If I'm an Evangelical."

Appendix 1

In 1999 in the article "Overlooked Shapers of Evangelicalism," George recognizes Basil Manly Sr. as someone whose impact has been underestimated.[15] Manly became known as the Baptist Bishop of Alabama. George views him as one of the most significant shapers of the Southern Baptist Tradition who has been overlooked. George points out that Manly was the second president of the University of Alabama. He was a preacher, a church planter, and he called for an education convention, which played a key part in the formation of the Southern Baptist Theological Seminary.

Selected Works by Timothy George: 2000s

In 2000 in the article "An Evangelical Reflection on Scripture and Tradition," George affirms that Evangelicals "can affirm the co-inherence of sacred Scripture and sacred Tradition, but not their coequality."[16] He outlines the key ideas and developments in the proper relationship between the supreme authority of the Bible and the role of tradition in the Christian faith and community.

In 2001 George contributed a chapter on Baptist theological identity to *Theologians of the Baptist Tradition*.[17] He includes five identity markers that characterize the wider Baptist tradition. The first is orthodox convictions. The second is evangelical heritage. The third is a reformed perspective. The fourth is Baptist distinctives, such as regenerate church membership and baptism on the basis of repentance and faith. The fifth is a confessional context.

In 2001 George offers a popular level summary of the doctrine of grace in his work, *Amazing Grace*, for the Southern Baptist Convention's Doctrine Study.[18] In chapter 1, he begins with "Our Gracious God." In chapter 2, he deals with "The Providence Mystery." In chapter 3, he covers the soteriological details involved in being "Saved by Grace." In chapter 4, he stresses that a theology of grace must produce a "Graceful Theology." In chapter 5, he explains the relationship between "Grace and the Great Commission." In chapter 6, he offers practical reflections on "Living by Grace."

In 2009 in *J. I. Packer and the Evangelical Future*, George describes Packer's influence on his life and ministry as a key figure of evangelicalism.[19]

15. George, "Overlooked Shapers of Evangelicalism," 76–77.
16. George, "Evangelical Reflection on Scripture," 184–207.
17. George, "Future of Baptist Theology," 1–10.
18. George, *Amazing Grace*.
19. George, *J. I. Packer*.

He also focuses on the definition of evangelicalism as "a renewal movement within historic Christian orthodoxy."[20] He maintains the importance of vital spirituality and sound theology.

In 2011 George contributes a chapter to *Evangelicals and Nicene Faith* as a tribute to Jaroslav Pelikan.[21] He claims that the deepest passion of Pelikan's soul was to tell the story of the Christian Tradition. He introduces readers to Pelikan's Slavic heritage and upbringing. He surveys Pelikan's love and appreciation for the grand scope of the Tradition. George admits that he never had Pelikan as a classroom teacher. He claims, however, "I was one of his students, as everyone seriously interested in Christian history has to be."[22]

In 2011 in *Reading Scripture with the Reformers*, George recounts the story of how the Bible secured the central place in the movement of reform in the sixteenth century that is known as the Reformation.[23] In Chapter 1, George gives an extensive autobiographical account of his time at Harvard Divinity School and his theological formation in regard to the conclusions that shape his historical theological commitments and methods as well as this work. Key people are introduced, such as antagonist Harvey Cox[24] and protagonists David Steinmetz and George Huntston Williams.

In 2011 in *Southern Baptists, Evangelicals and the Future of Denominationalism*, he wrote the chapter "The Faith, My Faith, and the Church's Faith."[25] George defined faith in three ways. The first way is to talk about the faith once delivered—the objective faith. The second is to talk about one's act of trust—subjective faith. The third way is to talk about the testimony of others' faith throughout the centuries. Each of these components of faith is important to understand and appreciate the task and place of historical theology.

In 2013 in the article, "Is Jesus a Baptist?," George introduces the idea of a "hierarchy of ecclesial realities."[26] He clarifies this by describing himself as a Protestant, an Evangelical, and a Baptist. He admits, however, that none of those labels defines his spiritual and ecclesial identity at its core.

---

20. George, "*Unde, Quonam, et Quemadmodum?*," 166.

21. George, "Delighted by Doctrine," 202–6.

22. George, "Delighted by Doctrine," 202.

23. George, *Reading Scripture with the Reformers*.

24. For a brief introduction to the work of Harvey Cox, see Garrett, *Baptist Theology*, 609–12.

25. George, "Faith, My Faith," 81–93.

26. George, "Is Jesus a Baptist?," para. 2.

Appendix 1

He writes, "Being an evangelical Protestant, a Baptist, indeed a Southern Baptist, are all important markers of my place within the community of faith, but there is a more primary confession I must make: I am a trinitarian Christian who by the grace of God belongs to the whole company of the redeemed through the ages."[27]

In 2013 in the work *Why We Belong: Evangelical Unity and Denominational Diversity*, George explains why he is a Baptist and an Evangelical.[28] He offers a descriptive autobiographical account of his early life in the Baptist church, his teenage years as a youth evangelist, and his formative time at Harvard Divinity School. He engages with the Bebbington definition of evangelicalism but offers his own diachronic account.

In 2014 George presents a profile of George Huntston Williams in "A Holy Calling: To Keep Truth Alive."[29] He emphasizes the "special task of the church historian was to make meaningful at least two articles of the creed: the *una sancta* and the *communio sanctorum*."[30]

In 2015 in the article "Remembering David Steinmetz's Quest to free the Church from Amnesia," George describes Steinmetz as one of the leading church historians of our time to combat the present theological amnesia and regain our collective Christian identity from the past.[31] He outlines Steinmetz in four ways. First, he viewed him as a beloved teacher. Steinmetz was a visiting professor when George was at Harvard Divinity School. Second, he referred to him as a pioneering scholar because of his work, "The Superiority of Pre-Critical Exegesis." Third, he viewed him as a Respecter of the Text because of the way he approached the Bible like a mystery novel. Fourth, he appreciated Steinmetz as a churchman committed to the United Methodist Church.

In 2015 in the article, "Jesus on Safari," George reflects on the legacy of his greatest intellectual mentor Jaroslav Pelikan.[32] George summarizes Pelikan's five-volume work on the Christian tradition as "what the church of Jesus Christ believes, teaches, and confesses on the basis of the Word of

---

27. George, "Is Jesus a Baptist?," para. 2.
28. George, "Why I Am an Evangelical," 93–109.
29. George, "Holy Calling."
30. George, "Holy Calling," para. 3.
31. George, "Remembering David Steinmetz's Quest."
32. George, "Jesus on Safari."

God."[33] George introduces readers to Pelikan's biography and significance in the landscape of Christian scholarship.

In 2016 in the article "In Honor of David Steinmetz," George celebrates the life and work of David Steinmetz.[34] He reflects on taking Steinmetz's course at Harvard Divinity School on "Calvin and the Reformed Tradition" and Steinmetz sitting on his doctoral examination. George would later teach a course at Beeson Divinity by the same name. He expresses appreciation for Steinmetz's work on pre-critical exegesis. He attributes the existence of *The Ancient Christian Commentary on Scripture* and *The Reformation Commentary on Scripture* to Steinmetz's theory of Biblical Interpretation.

In 2016 George recounts how through the mechanism of recovery and retrieval Tom Oden, prominent leader of the religious left, discovered orthodox Christianity in the early church figures.[35] He describes the extraordinary life[36] that he lived and his passion for Christian unity through classical Christian truths like the Trinity and Christology.[37]

In 2016 George titles an article "The Reformation, A Tragic Necessity," which he borrows from Jaroslav Pelikan.[38] He refers to Pelikan as "the greatest historian of Christian doctrine since Adolf von Harnack."[39] The phrase is taken from Pelikan's work, *The Riddle of Roman Catholicism*.[40] In the article, George affirms both the necessity and tragedy of the Reformation.

In 2017 in an article titled, "Baptists and Ecumenism: An Interview with Timothy George," George distinguishes between theological commitments and tests for fellowship.[41] He anticipates that the nature of the church will be the coming theological controversy. He explains what he means by "an ecumenism of conviction, not an ecumenism of accommodation."[42]

In 2017 during the five-hundred-year anniversary of the Reformation, George contributed a chapter, "Baptists and Calvin Today: The Importance of the Reformation for Baptists," to the book *Reformation 500*. George

---

33. George, "Jesus on Safari," para. 1.
34. George, "In Honor of David Steinmetz."
35. George, "Reversed Thunder."
36. For a biographical account see Oden, *Change of Heart*.
37. See Oden, *Classic Christianity*.
38. George, "Reformation."
39. George, "Reformation," para. 1.
40. Pelikan, *Riddle of Roman Catholicism*, 45.
41. George, "Baptists and Ecumenism," 89–92.
42. George, "Baptists and Ecumenism," 89–92.

Appendix 1

identifies five principles that Baptists can learn from John Calvin: Holy Scripture and the Living Christ, God-centered worship, the sovereignty of God in salvation, the World as theater of God's glory, and Christian unity.[43] Calvin did not seek unity by compromising truth, but rather he sought unity on the conviction of the truth.

Works Concerning Timothy George

James Leo Garrett and David Dockery offer tributes that recognize the importance of the work of Timothy George as an area deserving of attention and further study. Garrett is the Distinguished Professor Emeritus of Theology at Southwestern Baptist Theological Seminary. His work, *Baptist Theology: A Four-Century Study*, is a history of Christian theology in the Baptist tradition. Garrett writes an entire section about George in the chapter, "New Voices in Baptist Theology." He classifies George as an "Evangelical/Calvinist and Baptist Historical Theologian."

Dockery, James Earl Massey, and Robert Smith Jr. edited a volume of essays in honor of the life, leadership, and ministry of Timothy George titled *Worship, Tradition, and Engagement: Essays in Honor of Timothy George*. This volume addresses themes important to George, such as "The Gospel and Worship, the Church and Tradition, and Ministry and Engagement." In this work, Dockery offers a helpful introductory tribute to George that recognizes his contributions and offers a biographical sketch of his life and career.

---

43. George, "Baptists and Calvin Today," 45–54.

Appendix 2

Selected Works by Williams, Steinmetz, and Pelikan

A SURVEY OF PRIMARY and secondary works regarding George Huntston Williams, David Steinmetz, and Jaroslav Pelikan will provide the landscape where research will uncover each figure's biographical and professional context, historical and theological approach, and key thoughts that contribute to George's view.

Selected Works by George Huntston Williams

George Huntston Williams was the Winn Professor of Ecclesiastical History and was later appointed as the Hollis Chair of Divinity at Harvard Divinity School. Willams was Timothy George's mentor and thesis advisor during his graduate and doctoral studies. *The Radical Reformation* illustrates the approach of Williams to church history.[1] Williams approaches the task with seriousness and sympathy. He offers a rigorous and high-level examination. He also seeks to understand and appreciate the lesser known groups of the Reformation like the Anabaptists.

In 1982 Williams gave the lecture "In Defense of Church History" at Trinity Evangelical Divinity School which was later published in *The*

---

1. Williams, *Radical Reformation*.

Appendix 2

Contentious Triangle: Church, State, and University.[2] He defends church history as a theological discipline. He defines church history as "the history of the community of faith in time and space."[3] He distinguishes *church* history from *ecclesiastical* history, which is merely a subset of general history. He was concerned with the craft of history and the specific purpose of church history. He contributed the chapter, "Church History: From Historical Theology to the Theology of History," which is an overview and examination of church history and its theory and practice in North America in the Twentieth Century.[4]

Williams pioneered Ecumenical dialogues between Protestants and Catholics and encouraged collaboration for social justice. He wrote the first book in English about Pope John Paul II, *The Mind of John Paul II: Origins of His Thought and Action.*[5]

Selected Works by David Steinmetz

David Steinmetz was the professor of history of Christianity at Duke Divinity School. He was also a member of Timothy George's doctoral committee at Harvard. He was a visiting professor at Harvard Divinity School in 1977. Steinmetz's collection of essays titled *Taking the Long View: Christian Theology in Historical Perspective* includes his essay, "Superiority of Pre-Critical Exegesis."[6] This essay had a significant impact on Timothy George. George writes about the shaping effect of these essays on his understanding and practice of historical theology in his book *Reading Scripture with the Reformers.*

In 1968 Steinmetz published his first book *Misericordia Dei.*[7] In this work he sought to understand the theology of John Staupitz, who was Luther's monastic superior, in light of the theological context of the Middle Ages. This work originated as a dissertation at Harvard under the supervision of Heiko Oberman.

In 1971 Steinmetz first published the work *Reformers in the Wings.*[8] The work was updated and revised in 2000. It acts as an introduction to

2. Williams, "In Defense of Church History," 399–411.
3. Williams, "In Defense of Church History," 401.
4. Williams, "Church History," 147–80.
5. Williams, *Mind of John Paul II.*
6. Steinmetz, *Taking the Long View.*
7. Steinmetz, *Misericordia Dei.*
8. Steinmetz, *Reformers in the Wings.*

Reformation theology. Steinmetz facilitates this introduction by introducing reformers from four confessional families. He includes Catholic, Lutheran, Reformed, and Radical. Each chapter examines a debated theological issue in the sixteenth century in the context of a lesser known (in the wings) Reformation figure and story.

In 1986 Steinmetz published a series of essays in one volume titled *Luther in Context*.[9] He seeks to establish Luther in his intellectual and theological context rather than merely his social context. He laments that historians have primarily focused on the Reformation as social history rather than intellectual history. These essays present Luther in dialogue with the theological thinkers from the past and his own generation.

In 1995 Steinmetz published the first edition of *Calvin in Context*.[10] He acknowledges that much of the scholarship concerning the theology of John Calvin has not appropriately engaged his historical context and contemporaries. Thus, he seeks to better understand Calvin's theology by studying a range of primary sources, his Bible commentaries, and using a comparative method with Calvin's contemporaries.

Selected Works by Jaroslav Pelikan

Jaroslav Pelikan taught at Yale Divinity School as the Titus Street Professor of Ecclesiastical History until 1972 when he became sterling professor of history. He was Timothy George's greatest intellectual mentor through his writing, especially the five-volume work *The Christian Tradition: A History of the Development of Doctrine*.

Pelikan offers an intellectual history that revolves around the reception and reaction to the figure of Jesus in his work *Jesus Through the Centuries: His Place in the History of Culture*.[11] He evaluates the social, cultural, economic, and political values that are reflected in different times and the perception of Jesus within that period of time.

Pelikan engages the idea of change and development in Christian doctrine in his work *Development of Christian Doctrine: Some Historical Prolegomena*.[12] He offers three historical case studies. First, he presents Cyprian and original sin. Second, he examines Athanasius and the Virgin Mary.

---

9. Steinmetz, *Luther in Context*.
10. Steinmetz, *Calvin in Context*.
11. Pelikan, *Jesus Through the Centuries*.
12. Pelikan, *Development of Christian Doctrine*.

Third, he presents Hilary and the Holy Spirit. He considers two contributing factors in the development of doctrine: the theological reflection of the Christian thinker and the ecclesiological assimilation of the Christian community.

Pelikan introduces solutions to the problem of change and the relationship between history and theology in Christian doctrine in the work *Historical Theology: Continuity and Change in Christian Doctrine*.[13] He examines the views of Vincent of Lerins, Abelard, Aquinas, and Adolf von Harnack before offering his own definition and method of historical theology.

In the work *Whose Bible Is It? A History of the Scriptures through the Ages*, Pelikan traces the Bible's form from the oral narrative to the texts in Hebrew and Greek.[14] He then follows its form from the autographs to modern versions. He considers the positive impact that technology like the printing press and religious events like the Protestant Reformation have had on the appreciation and use of the Bible. He explores how different faith traditions view and value the Holy Bible.

In the work *Credo: Historical and Theological Guide to Creeds and Confessions of Faith in the Christian Tradition*, Pelikan surveys the historic creeds of the Christian church.[15] Areas of special interest in this volume are his definition of the faith as well as his focus on the teaching of the church and its doctrines. The entire work is an example of historical theology performed at the highest level.

---

13. Pelikan, *Historical Theology*.
14. Pelikan, *Whose Bible Is It?*.
15. Pelikan, *Credo*.

Bibliography

Abbott, Walter. *The Documents of Vatican II.* New York: Guild, 1966.
Adams, James. "George Huntston Williams: A Portrait." In *Continuity and Discontinuity in Church History: Essays Presented to George Huntston Williams on the Occasion of His 65th Birthday*, edited by F. Forrester Church and Timothy George, 1–17. Lieden: Brill, 1979.
Allen, Jason K. "Panel Discussion: Drummond Lectures with Timothy and Christian George." Lecture given at Midwestern Seminary on March 3, 2016. https://jasonkallen.com/2016/03/2901/.
Allen, Michael, and Scott Swain. "Introduction to New Studies in Dogmatics." *Common Places* (blog), April 16, 2015. https://zondervanacademic.com/blog/common-places-introduction-to-new-studies-in-dogmatics/.
———. *Reformed Catholicity: The Promise of Retrieval for Theology and Biblical Interpretation*. Grand Rapids: Baker Academic, 2015.
Allison, Gregg R. *Historical Theology: An Introduction to Christian Doctrine*. Grand Rapids: Zondervan, 2011.
Aquinas, Thomas. *Summa Theologica Volume II: Part II-II*. Translated by Fathers of the English Dominican Province. United Kingdom: Bournes, Oates and Washbourne, 1922.
Bainton, Roland. *Here I Stand: A Life of Martin Luther*. New York: Abingdon-Cokesbury, 1950.
Barrett, Matthew. "Reading Scripture with the Reformers: Interview with Timothy George." *Credo Magazine* 1.1 (2011) 68–71.
Bebbington, David. *Baptists through the Centuries: A History of a Global People*. 2nd ed. Waco: Baylor University Press, 2018.
Beeson Divinity School. *Beeson Divinity School Bulletin 2019–20*. Birmingham, AL: Samford University, 2019.
———. "Confession of Faith." In *Beeson Divinity School Bulletin 2019–2020*, 3. Birmingham: Samford University, 2019.

Bibliography

———. "Curriculum." In *Beeson Bulletin 2019-2020*, 41–52. Birmingham: Samford University, 2019.

Berardino, Angelo, ed. *We Believe in One Holy Catholic and Apostolic Church*. Ancient Christian Doctrine. Downers Grove: IVP Academic, 2010.

Berry, Everett, and Winston Hottman. "Baptists and Ecumenism: An Interview with Timothy George." *Criswell Theological Review* 14 (2017) 89–92. http://www.centerforbaptistrenewal.com/blog/2017/4/6/baptists-and-ecumenism-a-discussion-with-timothy-george.

Bracey, Matthew Steven. "Interview with Timothy George." http://www.helwyssocietyforum.com/interview-with-timothy-george/.

Braude, Ann. "A Short Half-Century: Fifty Years of Women at Harvard Divinity School." *Harvard Theological Review* 99.4 (2006) 369–80.

Bray, Gerald. *God Has Spoken: A History of Christian Theology*. Wheaton: Crossway, 2014.

Briggs, Kenneth. "Linguistics Are the Key to Unique Life's Work." *New York Times* 2 (1979), sec. C, 5.

Broek, Allison. "Rallying the Right-to-Lifers: Grassroots Religion and Politics in the Building of a Broad-based Right-to-Life Movement, 1960–1984." PhD diss., Boston College, 2018.

Buschart, William David. "Perspectives on Christian Doctrine in the Work of Jaroslav Pelikan: His Vindication of the Christian Tradition." PhD diss., Drew University, 1988.

Calhoun, Robert. Review of *The Christian Tradition: A History of the Development of Doctrine. Vol. 1, The Emergence of the Catholic Tradition (100–600)*, by Jaroslav Pelikan. *Journal of the American Academy of Religion* 40 (1972) 501.

Chute, Anthony, et al. *The Baptist Story: From English Sect to Global Movement*. Nashville: B&H Academic, 2015.

Conger, Yves. *Divided Christendom*. London: Centenary, 1939.

"Contested Ground." http://www.sbts.edu/about/history/contested-ground-1981-1993/.

Cox, Harvey. *Turning East*. New York: Simon & Schuster, 1977.

"David S. Dockery." https://swbts.edu/staff/david-s-dockery/.

"David Steinmetz Dies at 79." https://divinity.duke.edu/news/david-steinmetz-dies-79.

Dever, Mark. "A Catholic Church: Galatians 3:26–29," In *The Church: One, Holy, Catholic, and Apostolic*, edited by Richard D. Phillips et al., 71–72. Phillipsburg: P&R, 2004.

———. *The Church*. Nashville: B&H Academic, 2012.

———. "Lose the Church, Lose the Gospel." In *Worship, Tradition, and Engagement: Essays in Honor of Timothy George*, edited by David S. Dockery et al., 35–47. Eugene, OR: Pickwick, 2018.

DeVine, Mark. "An Unacknowledged Heritage." In *Worship, Tradition, and Engagement: Essays in Honor of Timothy George*, edited by David Dockery et al., 183–99. Eugene, OR: Pickwick, 2018.

Dockery, David S. "Foreword." In *When Doctrine Divides the People of God: An Evangelical Approach to Theological Diversity*, by Rhyne R. Putman, 11–15. Wheaton: Crossway, 2020.

———. "Timothy George: An Introductory Tribute." In *Worship, Tradition, and Engagement: Essays in Honor of Timothy George*, edited by David S. Dockery et al., 1–17. Eugene, OR: Pickwick, 2018.

Dockery, David S., et al., eds. *Worship, Tradition, and Engagement: Essays in Honor of Timothy George*. Eugene, OR: Pickwick, 2018.

Bibliography

Duesing, Jason, ed. *Upon This Rock*. Nashville: B&H Publishing, 2010.
Ebeling, Gerhard. *The Word of God and Tradition: Historical Studies Interpreting the Divisions of Christianity*. Translated by S. H. Hooke. London: Collins, 1968.
Edwards, Mark. Review of *Calvin in Context*, by David Steinmetz. *The Journal of Religion* (1997) 628.
Emerson, Matthew, and R. Lucas Stamps. "Baptists and the Catholicity of the Church: Toward an Evangelical Baptist Catholicity." *Journal of Baptist Studies* 7 (2015) 42–66.
Emerson, Matthew, et al., eds. *Baptists and the Christian Tradition: Toward an Evangelical Baptist Catholicity*. Nashville: B&H Academic, 2020.
Emerton, Ephraim. "A Definition of Church History." *Papers of the American Society of Church History* 7 (1923) 53–68.
———. "The Study of Church History." *Unitarian Review and Religious Magazine* 19 (1883) 1.
Fea, John. *Why Study History? Reflecting on the Importance of the Past*. Grand Rapids: Baker Academic, 2013.
Finn, Nathan. *History: A Student's Guide*. Wheaton: Crossway, 2016.
Forstman, Jack. Review of *The Christian Tradition: A History of the Development of Doctrine*. Vol. 1, *The Emergence of the Catholic Tradition (100–600)*, by Jaroslav Pelikan. *Journal of Religion* 55 (1975) 96–97.
Fox, William L. "Honoring the C Student." https://web.archive.org/web/20210209032640/https://www.stlawu.edu/president/honoring-c-student.
Garrett, James Leo. *Baptist Theology: A Four Century Study*. Macon, GA: Mercer University Press, 2009.
———. *Systematic Theology*. Vol. 1. *Biblical, Historical, and Evangelical*. 4th ed. Eugene, OR: Wipf & Stock, 1990.
"George H. Williams: Renewing Religion at Harvard." *Harvard Square Library*. https://www.harvardsquarelibrary.org/wp-content/uploads/2017/03/Great-American-Events-and-Universalists-George-Huntston-Williams.pdf.
George, Timothy. *Amazing Grace: God's Pursuit, Our Response*. 2nd ed. Wheaton: Crossway, 2011.
———. "Baptist Renewal." *Beeson Podcast*, January 22, 2019. https://www.beesondivinity.com/podcast/2019/Baptist-Renewal.
———. "A Baptist Theologian: Reflections on Anglicanism." In *The Future of Orthodox Anglicanism*, edited by Gerald McDermott, 227–45. Wheaton: Crossway, 2020.
———. "Baptists and Calvin Today: The Importance of the Reformation for Baptists." In *Reformation 500*, edited by Ray Van Neste and J. Michael Garrett, 45–54. Nashville: B&H Publishing, 2017.
———. *Baptists at Beeson*. Birmingham, AL: Beeson Divinity School, 2019.
———. "Barmen and the Baptists." *Beeson Podcast*, April 5, 2011. https://www.beesondivinity.com/podcast/audio/beeson-podcast-episode-024-mohler.mp3.
———. "Between the Pope and Billy Graham: Evangelicals and Catholics in Dialogue." In *Pilgrims on the Sawdust Trail: Evangelical Ecumenism and the Quest for Christian Identity*, edited by Timothy George, 125–37. Grand Rapids: Baker Academic, 2004.
———. "The Blessed Evangelical Mary." *Christianity Today*, December 1, 2003. https://www.christianitytoday.com/ct/2003/december/1.34.html.
———. "The Blessed Virgin Mary: An Evangelical Perspective." In *Mary, Mother of God*, edited by Carl E. Braaten and Robert W. Jenson, 100–122. Grand Rapids: Eerdmans, 2004.

---. "Catholics and Baptists Together." *Christianity Today*, February 13, 2013. https://www.christianitytoday.com/ct/2013/january-february/catholics-and-baptists-together.html.

---. "Catholics and Evangelicals in the Trenches." *Christianity Today*, May 16, 1994. https://www.christianitytoday.com/ct/1994/may-16/editorials.html.

---. "Church History as a Theological Discipline." https://www.biblicaltraining.org/church-history-theological-discipline/theology-reformers.

---. "Church History as a Theological Discipline." Lecture given at Beeson Divinity School, Samford University in Birmingham, Alabama in 2011. In *Lectures on Church History*, disc 1, Beeson Media Archive, 2013. 14 CDs.

---. "The Church of the Undivided Christ." *Ecumenical Trends* 42.11 (2013) 1.

---. "A Conversation on Theology." *Beeson Podcast*, November, 5, 2018. https://www.beesondivinity.com/podcast/2018/transcripts/Beeson-Podcast-Episode-417-vanhoozer.txt.

---. "Dean's Installation." *Journal of Beeson Divinity School* (2008) 3.

---. "Defending Life." *Beeson Podcast*, March 22, 2011. https://www.beesondivinity.com/podcast/audio/beeson-podcast-episode-022-beckwith.mp3.

---. "Delighted by Doctrine." *Christian History & Biography* 91 (2006) 43–45.

---. "Delighted by Doctrine." *Christianity Today*, September 15, 2006. https://www.christianitytoday.com/ct/2006/septemberweb-only/137-53.0.html.

---. "Delighted by Doctrine: A Tribute to Jaroslav Pelikan." In *Evangelicals and Nicene Faith: Reclaiming the Apostolic Witness*, edited by Timothy George, 202–6. Beeson Divinity Studies. Grand Rapids: Baker, 2011.

---. "Dogma beyond Anathema: Historical Theology in the Service of the Church." *Review and Expositor* 84.4 (1987) 691–713.

---. "ECT at Twenty." *Beeson Podcast*, November 17, 2015. https://www.beesondivinity.com/podcast/audio/beeson-podcast-episode-262-guarino_01.mp3.

---. "Ecumenism: A Personal Journey." *Beeson Podcast*, September 5, 2017. https://www.beesondivinity.com/podcast/2017/Ecumenism-A-personal-journey.

---. "Ecumenism after 50 Years." *First Things* (blog), December 1, 2014. https://www.firstthings.com/web-exclusives/2014/12/ecumenism-after-50-years.

---. "An Evangelical Reflection on Scripture and Tradition." *Pro Ecclesia* 912 (2000) 184–207.

---. "Evangelical Theology in North American Contexts." In *The Cambridge Companion to Evangelical Theology*, edited by Timothy Larsen and Daniel J. Treier, 275–92. Cambridge: Cambridge University Press, 2007.

---. "Evangelicals and Catholics Together: An Evangelical Assessment." *Christianity Today*, December 8, 1997. https://www.christianitytoday.com/ct/1997/december8/7te034.html.

---, ed. *Evangelicals and Nicene Faith: Reclaiming the Apostolic Witness*. Beeson Divinity Studies. Grand Rapids: Baker, 2011.

---. "Evangelicals and the Great Tradition." *First Things* 175 (2007) 19–21.

---. "Evangelicals and the Mother of God." *First Things* 170 (2007) 20–26.

---. "Evangelicals and the Present Ecumenical Moment." In *Critical Issues in Ecclesiology: Essays in Honor of Carl E. Braaten*, edited by Alberto L. García and Susan K. Wood, 44–67. Grand Rapids: Eerdmans, 2011.

---. "Evangelicalism." *Modern Reformation* 17.7 (2008) 23.

Bibliography

———. "The Faith, My Faith, and the Church's Faith." In *Southern Baptists, Evangelicals, and the Future of Denominationalism*, edited by Jerry Tidwell et al., 81–94. Nashville: B&H Academic, 2011.

———. "Foreword." In *Baptists and the Christian Tradition: Toward an Evangelical Baptist Catholicity*, edited by Matthew Emerson et al., xv–xvii. Nashville: B&H Publishing, 2020.

———. "Foreword." In *The Pastor Theologian: Resurrecting an Ancient Vision*, by Gerald Hiestand and Todd Wilson, 7–8. Grand Rapids: Zondervan, 2015.

———. "The Future of Baptist Theology." In *Theologians of the Baptist Tradition*, edited by Timothy George and David S. Dockery, 1–10. Nashville: Broadman & Holman, 2001.

———. "George Huntston Williams: A Historian for All Seasons." *American Journal of Theology and Philosophy* 7.2 (1986) 75–93.

———. "George Huntston Williams: A Historian for All Seasons." In *The Contentious Triangle: Church, State and University: A Festschrift in Honor of Professor George Huntston Williams*, edited by Rodney L. Peterson and Calvin Augustine Pater, 15-34. Sixteenth Century Essays & Studies 51. Kirksville: Thomas Jefferson University Press, 1999.

———. "The Gift of Salvation." *First Things* 79 (1998) 2–3.

———. "The Great Shapers of Evangelicalism in the 20th Century." *Beeson Podcast*, May 2, 2017. https://www.beesondivinity.com/podcast/2017/audio/beeson-podcast-episode-338-woodbridge.mp3.

———. "A Holy Calling: To Keep Truth Alive." *First Things* (blog), March 10, 2014. http://www.firstthings.com/web-exclusives/2014/03/a-holy-calling-to-keep-truth-alive.

———. "If I'm an Evangelical, What Am I?" *Christianity Today*, August 9, 1999. https://www.christianitytoday.com/ct/1999/august9/9t9062.html.

———. "In Honor of David Steinmetz." *First Things* (blog), January 11, 2016. https://www.firstthings.com/web-exclusives/2016/01/in-honor-of-david-steinmetz.

———. "In the Shadow of the Clinic." *Beeson Podcast*, May 21, 2013. https://www.beesondivinity.com/podcast/audio/beeson-podcast-episode-134-childs.mp3.

———. "Interpretation, History, and the Ecumenical Movement: Response to Jeffrey Gros." *Ecumenical Trends* 16.7 (1987) 131–32.

———. "Is Jesus a Baptist?" *First Things* (blog), August 12, 2013. http://www.firstthings.com/onthesquare/2013/08/is-jesus-a-baptist.

———. "Is Jesus a Baptist?" In *Southern Baptist Identity: An Evangelical Denomination Faces the Future*, edited by David Dockery, 89–104. Wheaton: Crossway, 2009.

———. "Jesus on Safari." *First Things* (blog), January 26, 2015. https://www.firstthings.com/web-exclusives/2015/01/jesus-on-safari.

———. "John Paul II: An Appreciation." *Pro Ecclesia* 14.3 (2005) 267–70.

———. *John Robinson and the English Separatist Tradition*. Macon, GA: Mercer University Press, 1982.

———. "A Journey into the Unknown." *Christianity Today* 59.6 (2015) 70–73.

———. "A Life Fit for Eternity." https://www.beesondivinity.com/blog/2018/george-a-life-fit-for-eternity.

———. "The Manhattan Declaration." *Beeson Podcast*, October 25, 2010. https://www.beesondivinity.com/podcast/2010/The-Manhattan-Declaration.

———. "My Own Pilgrim's Progress." *Christianity Today*, August 19, 2015. https://www.christianitytoday.com/ct/2015/july-august/my-own-pilgrims-progress.html.

Bibliography

———. "My Top Five Classics of Reformation Studies." *Christianity Today*, September 3, 2009. https://www.christianitytoday.com/history/2009/september/my-top-five-classics-of-reformation-studies.html.

———. *The New American Commentary*. Vol. 30, *Galatians*. Nashville: Broadman & Holman, 1994.

———. "Our Francis, Too." *Christianity Today*, June 4, 2013. https://www.christianitytoday.com/ct/2013/june/our-francis-too.html.

———. "Overlooked Shapers of Evangelicalism." *The Southern Baptist Journal Theology* 3.1 (1999) 76–77.

———. "Partly Fearing, Partly Hoping: Evangelicals, Southern Baptists, and the Quest for a New Consensus." *Perspectives in Religious Studies* 17 (1990) 167–72.

———. "Pope John Paul II." *Beeson Podcast*, July 5, 2011. https://www.beesondivinity.com/podcast/audio/beeson-podcast-episode-037-weigel.mp3.

———. "Preface." In *Galatians: The Christian Standard Commentary*, 14–17. Nashville: B&H Publishing, 2020.

———. "Profiles of Expository Preaching." *The Southern Baptist Journal of Theology* 3.2 (1999) 89–91.

———. "The Promise of Benedict XVI." *Christianity Today*, May 26, 2005. https://www.christianitytoday.com/ct/2005/june/19.49.html.

———. "Promoting Renewal, Not Tribalism." *Christianity Today*, June 17, 1996. https://www.christianitytoday.com/ct/1996/june17/6t7014.html.

———. *Reading Scripture with the Reformers*. Downers Grove: InterVarsity, 2011.

———. "The Reformation, a Tragic Necessity." *First Things* (blog), July 11, 2016. https://www.firstthings.com/web-exclusives/2016/07/the-reformation-a-tragic-necessity.

———. "The Reformation Roots of the Baptist Tradition." *Review and Expositor* 86.1 (1989) 9–22.

———. "Remembering David Steinmetz's Quest to Free the Church from Amnesia." *Christianity Today*, December 14, 2015. https://www.christianitytoday.com/ct/2015/december-web-only/remembering-david-steinmetz-quest-to-free-church-from-amnes.html.

———. "Remembering George Huntston Williams." *Beeson Podcast*, December, 5, 2017. https://www.beesondivinity.com/podcast/2017/transcripts/JimSmith.podcast.edited.txt.

———. "Remembering Leading Reformation Scholar, David C. Steinmetz." https://www.ivpress.com/press-releases/2015/remembering-leading-reformation-scholar-david-c-steinmetz.

———. "The Responsibility of the Local Church." https://www.capitolhillbaptist.org/sermon/the-responsibility-of-the-local-church/.

———. "Retrieval for the Sake of Renewal." *First Things* (blog), May 15, 2017. https://www.firstthings.com/web-exclusives/2017/05/retrieval-for-the-sake-of-renewal.

———. "Reversed Thunder: A Tribute to Thomas C. Oden (1931–2016)." *Christianity Today*, December 13, 2016. https://www.christianitytoday.com/ct/2016/december-web-only/reversed-thunder-tribute-to-thomas-c-oden-1931-2016.html.

———. "A Right Strawy Epistle: Reformation Perspectives on James." *Review and Expositor* 83.3 (1986) 369–82. Reprinted in *The Southern Baptist Journal of Theology* 4.3 (2000) 20–31.

———. "Sharp-Elbow Ecumenism." *Beeson Podcast*, May 5, 2015. https://www.beesondivinity.com/podcast/audio/beeson-podcast-episode-233-reno_01.mp3.

Bibliography

———. "Southern Baptist Ghosts." *First Things* 93 (1999) 18–24.
———. "Southern Baptist Relations with Other Protestants." *Baptist History and Heritage* 25.3 (1990) 24–34.
———. "Systematic Theology at Southern Seminary." *Review and Expositor* 82.11 (1985) 31–47.
———. "A Theological Introduction." In *Evangelicals and Catholics Together at Twenty*, edited by Timothy George and Thomas Guarino, xvi–xxxvi. Grand Rapids: Brazos, 2015.
———. *Theology of the Reformers*. Rev. ed., Nashville: B&H Publishing, 2013.
———. "A Thicker Kind of Mere." *First Things* (blog), May 18, 2015. https://www.firstthings.com/web-exclusives/2015/05/a-thicker-kind-of-mere.
———. "Three Marks of the Church." *Proclaim* 15.1 (1984) 28–30.
———. "Toward an Evangelical Ecclesiology." In *Catholics and Evangelicals: Do They Share a Common Future?*, edited by Thomas P. Rausch, 122–48. New York: Paulist, 2000.
———. "Twenty Years of Gratitude." *Journal of Beeson Divinity School* (2008) 1–2.
———. "*Unde, Quonam, et Quemadmodum*? Learning Latin (and Other Things) from J. I. Packer." In *J. I. Packer and the Evangelical Future: The Impact of His Life and Thought*, edited by Timothy George, 163–70. Ada: Baker Academic, 2009.
———. "*Unitatis Redintegratio* after 50 Years: A Protestant Reading." *Pontifical Council for Promoting Christian Unity: Information Service* 144 (2014) 69–76.
———. "*Unitatis Redintegratio* after Fifty Years: A Protestant Reading." *Pro Ecclesia* 25 (2016) 53–70.
———. "Unity." In *Evangelicals and Catholics Together at Twenty*, edited by Timothy George and Thomas Guarino, 1–5. Grand Rapids: Brazos, 2015.
———. "Unplanned." *Beeson Podcast*, October 1, 2013. https://www.beesondivinity.com/podcast/audio/beeson-podcast-episode-153-johnson_01.mp3.
———. "Vatican 2: Semper Reformanda." *Beeson Podcast*, November 21, 2017. https://www.beesondivinity.com/podcast/2017/Vatican-2-Semper-Reformanda.
———. "Vatican II and Christian Unity." *Beeson Podcast*, July 18, 2017. https://www.beesondivinity.com/podcast/2017/Vatican-Two-and-Christian-Unity.
———. "What Belongs to God, What Belongs to Caesar: A Personal Reflection on The Manhattan Declaration." In *Life, Marriage, and Religious Liberty: What Belongs to God, What Belongs to Caesar*, by David Dockery, xiii–xviii. New York: Fidelis, 2019.
———. "What Do the Baptists Stand For?" *Beeson Podcast*, May 3, 2011. https://www.beesondivinity.com/podcast/audio/beeson-podcast-episode-028-coffey.mp3.
———. "What I'd Like to Tell the Pope about the Church." *Christianity Today*, June 15, 1998. https://www.christianitytoday.com/ct/1998/june15/8t7041.html.
———. "What the Reformers Thought They Were Doing." *Modern Age* (2017) 17–26.
———. "What We Mean When We Say It's True." *Christianity Today*, October 23, 1995. https://www.christianitytoday.com/ct/1995/october23/what-we-mean-when-we-say-its-true.html.
———. "What Were We Thinking? Looking Back on 25 Years." *Beeson Magazine*, 2013. https://www.beesondivinity.com/files/beeson-magazine-2013.pdf.
———. "Why I Am an Evangelical and a Baptist." In *Why We Belong: Evangelical Unity and Denominational Diversity*, edited by Anthony L. Chute et al., 93–109. Wheaton: Crossway, 2013.

Bibliography

———. "Why We Still Need Luther." *Christianity Today*, October 28, 1996. https://www.christianitytoday.com/ct/1996/october28/6tc013.html.

George, Timothy, and Dockery, David. *The Great Tradition of Christian Thinking: A Student's Guide, Reclaiming the Christian Intellectual Tradition*. Wheaton: Crossway, 2012.

Green, Jay. *Christian Historiography: Five Rival Versions*. Waco: Baylor University Press, 2015.

Guarino, Thomas. "Tradition and Doctrinal Development: Can Vincent of Lerins Still Teach the Church?" *Theological Studies* 67 (2006) 34–72.

———. "Vatican II and 'Evangelicals and Catholics Together: A Roman Catholic Perspective.'" In *Worship, Tradition, and Engagement: Essays in Honor of Timothy George*, edited by David Dockery, 247–61. Eugene, OR: Pickwick, 2018.

Hanna, Christopher R. Interview of Timothy George, Distinguished Professor of Divinity. Birmingham, AL, November, 30, 2017.

Hansen, Collin. "Timothy George and the Leadership That Lifts." *The Gospel Coalition*, April 4, 2019, https://www.thegospelcoalition.org/article/timothy-george-leadership-lifts/.

Harbison, E. Harris. *Christianity and History*. Princeton: Princeton University Press, 1964.

"Harold Grimm Prize." https://sixteenthcentury.org/harold-grimm-prize/.

Hatch, Nathan O. "Sola Scriptura and Novus Ordo Seclorum." In *The Bible in America: Essays in Cultural History*, edited by Nathan O. Hatch and Mark A. Noll, 59–78. New York: Oxford University Press, 1982.

Hehier, J. Bryan. "Professor George Huntston Williams: A Catholic Tribute." In *The Contentious Triangle: Church, State and University*, edited by Rodney L. Peterson and Calvin Augustine Pater, 347–57. Sixteenth Century Essays & Studies 51. Kirksville: Thomas Jefferson University Press, 1999.

Henn, William. "The Hierarchy of Truths Twenty Years Later." *Theological Studies* 48 (1987) 439–71.

Henry, Patrick, ed. *Schools of Thought in the Christian Tradition*. Philadelphia: Fortress, 1984.

Hinze, Bradford. Review of *Vindication of Tradition*, by Jaroslav Pelikan. *Journal of Religion* 66 (1986) 109.

"Historical and Doctrinal Studies." https://www.beesondivinity.com/master-of-divinity.

Horton, Michael. "A Review of The Manhattan Declaration." *White Horse Inn* (blog), January 12, 2009. https://www.whitehorseinn.org/2009/12/a-review-of-the-manhattan-declaration/.

Hotchkiss, Valerie. "Bibliography of Jaroslav Pelikan, 1946–2005." In *Orthodoxy and Western Culture: Essays in Honor of the 80th Birthday of Jaroslav Pelikan*, edited by Valerie Hotchkiss and Patrick Henry, 185–231. Crestwood: St. Vladimir's Press, 2005.

Hunt, Dave. "The Gospel Betrayed." *The Berean Call* (blog), May 1, 1994. https://www.thebereancall.org/content/gospel-betrayed.

Hutchison, William, et al. "Memorial Minute for George H. Williams." *Harvard Gazette*, n.d. https://news.harvard.edu/gazette/story/2003/03/memorial-minute-for-george-h-williams/.

Ingalls, Zoe. "Yale's Jaroslav Pelikan: 'Bilingual' Scholar of Christian Tradition." *Chronicle of Higher Education* 26 (1983) 4.

John XXIII, Pope. "Gaudet Mater Ecclesia." *Acta Apostolicae Sedis* 54 (1962) 786–96.

Bibliography

Jowett, Benjamin. "On the Interpretation of Scripture." In *Essays and Reviews*, 330–433. 7th ed. London: Longman, Green, Longman & Roberts, 1861.

Kidd, Thomas. *Who Is an Evangelical? The History of a Movement in Crisis*. New Haven: Yale University Press, 2019.

Kingdon, Robert. "Peter Martyr Vermigli and the Marks of the True Church." In *Continuity and Discontinuity in Church History: Essays Presented to George Huntston Williams on the Occasion of His 65th Birthday*, edited by F. Forrester Church and Timothy George, 198–214. Lieden: Brill, 1979.

Knox, Marv. "Seminary Presidents Decry Samford's Divinity School." http://media.sbhla.org.s3.amazonaws.com/6537,29-Feb-1988.PDF.

Köstenberger, Andreas. Review of *Biblical Interpretation in the Era of the Reformation: Essays Presented to David C. Steinmetz in Honor of His Sixtieth Birthday*, edited by Richard Muller and John Thompson. *Faith & Mission* (1998) 107.

Lane, Anthony. Review of *Biblical Interpretation in the Era of the Reformation: Essays Presented to David C. Steinmetz in Honor of His Sixtieth Birthday*, edited by Richard Muller and John Thompson. *The Journal of Ecclesiastical History* (1999) 158.

Lewis, C. S. "Preface." In *Mere Christianity*, vii–xvi. New York: HarperCollins, 2015.

Lewis, W. H., ed. *Letters of C. S. Lewis*. New York: Harcourt, Brace & World, 1966.

Littell, Franklin. "The Periodization of History." In *Continuity and Discontinuity in Church History: Essays Presented to George Huntston Williams on the Occasion of His 65th Birthday*, edited by F. Forrester Church and Timothy George, 18–30. Lieden: Brill, 1979.

MacArthur, John. "The Manhattan Declaration." *Grace to You* (blog), November 24, 2009. https://www.gty.org/library/articles/A390/the-manhattan-declaration.

MacCulloch, Diarmaid. Review of *Taking the Long View: Christian Theology in Historical Perspective*, by David Steinmetz. *The Journal of Ecclesiastical History* 64 (2013) 563.

Manetsch, Scott. "John Calvin and the Construction of a Confessional Church a Case Study for Evangelicals." In *Worship, Tradition, and Engagement: Essays in Honor of Timothy George*, edited by David S. Dockery et al., 165–82. Eugene, OR: Pickwick, 2018.

McBeth, Leon. *The Baptist Heritage: Four Centuries of Baptist Witness*. Nashville: Broadman, 1987.

McKee, Elsie. Review of *Biblical Interpretation in the Era of the Reformation: Essays Presented to David C. Steinmetz in Honor of His Sixtieth Birthday*, edited by Richard Muller and John Thompson. *The Journal of Religion* (1999) 289.

McKim, Donald. Review of *Calvin in Context*, by David Steinmetz. *Religious Studies Review* 22 (1996): 349.

McGrath, Alister E. *Historical Theology: An Introduction to the History of Christian Thought*. 2nd ed. New York: Wiley-Blackwell, 2012.

Mohler, Albert. "The Church and Pastor-Theologians." In *Worship, Tradition, and Engagement: Essays in Honor of Timothy George*, edited by David S. Dockery et al., 279–91. Eugene, OR: Pickwick, 2018.

Mouw, Richard. Review of *Calvin in Context*, by David Steinmetz. *Pro Ecclesia* (1998) 370.

Muller, Richard, and John Thompson, eds. *Biblical Interpretation in the Era of the Reformation: Essays Presented to David C. Steinmetz in Honor of His Sixtieth Birthday*. Grand Rapids: Eerdmans, 1996.

Musgraves, Evan. "Founding Saints of Beeson Divinity School." *Beeson Magazine*, May 29, 2019. https://www.beesondivinity.com/blog/2019/founding-saints-of-beeson.

Bibliography

———. Interview of Timothy George. Samford University Oral History Collection. https://www.samford.edu/departments/oral-history/projects/faculty/Timothy-George-Interview.

Nelson, David, and Charles Raith. *Ecumenism: A Guide for the Perplexed.* Guides for the Perplexed. New York: Bloomsbury, 2017.

Nestingen, James. Review of *Luther in Context*, by David Steinmetz. *Interpretation* 42 (1988) 305–7.

Newman, Albert Henry. *A Manual of Church History.* Philadelphia: American Baptist Publication Society, 1903.

Nichols, James Hastings. "The Art of Church History." *Church History* 20 (1951) 3–9.

Noll, Mark. "The Doctrine Doctor." *Christianity Today*, December 1, 2004. https://www.christianitytoday.com/ct/2004/decemberweb-only/12-27-42.0.html.

———. Review of *Vindication of Tradition*, by Jaroslav Pelikan. *TSF Bulletin* 10.2 (1986) 44.

Nunnelley, William. "$38.8 Million Ralph Beeson Bequest to Samford Largest in Alabama History." http://media.sbhla.org.s3.amazonaws.com/7061,19-Nov-1990.pdf.

Nunnelley, William, and Marv Knox. "Samford to Start Divinity School." http://media.sbhla.org.s3.amazonaws.com/6529,12-Feb-1988.pdf.

Nygren, Anders. *Agape and Eros.* Translated by Philip S. Watson. Philadelphia: Westminster, 1953.

Oden, Thomas. *A Change of Heart: A Personal and Theological Memoir.* Downers Grove: IVP Academic, 2014.

———. *Classic Christianity: A Systematic Theology.* New York: HarperOne, 2009.

Olson, Roger. *The Story of Christian Theology: Twenty Centuries of Tradition Reform.* Downers Grove: IVP Academic, 1999.

Ortlund, Gavin. *Finding the Right Hills to Die On: The Case for Theological Triage.* Wheaton: Crossway, 2020.

Packer, James, and Thomas Oden. *One Faith: The Evangelical Consensus.* Downers Grove: InterVarsity, 2004.

———. "Why I Signed It." *Christianity Today*, December 12, 1994. https://www.christianitytoday.com/ct/1994/december12/j-i-packer-why-i-signed-evangelical-and-catholics-together.html.

Padilla, Kristen. "Samford's Beeson Divinity School Founding Dean to Step Down in 2019." https://www.samford.edu/news/2018/05/Samford-Beeson-Divinity-School-Founding-Dean-to-Step-Down-in-2019.

Pelikan, Jaroslav. *Bach Among the Theologians.* Philadelphia: Fortress, 1986.

———. "Beyond Bellarmine and Harnack: The Present Task of the History of Dogma." *Theology Digest* 16 (1968) 299–309.

———. "Catholics in America." *New Republic* 142 (1960) 15.

———. "The Christian Tradition." *New Yorker*, Febuary 2, 1981.

———. *The Christian Tradition: A History of the Development of Doctrine.* 5 vols. Chicago: University of Chicago Press, 1971.

———. *Credo: Historical and Theological Guide to Creeds and Confessions of Faith in the Christian Tradition.* New Haven: Yale University Press, 2003.

———. *Development of Christian Doctrine: Some Historical Prolegomena.* New Haven: Yale University Press, 1969.

———. "An Essay on the Development of Christian Doctrine." *Church History* 35 (1966) 3–12.

Bibliography

———. "A First Generation Anselmian, Guibert of Nogent." In *Continuity and Discontinuity in Church History: Essays Presented. to George Huntston Williams*, edited by F. Forrester Church and Timothy George, 71–82. Leiden: Brill, 1979.

———. "Form and Tradition in Worship: A Theological Interpretation." In *The First Liturgical Institute*, 11–27. Valparaiso: Valparaiso University Press, 1950.

———. *From Luther to Kierkegaard: A Study in the History of Theology*. 2nd ed. St. Louis: Concordia, 1963.

———. "Historical Theology: A Presentation." *Criterion* 10 (1971) 26–27.

———. *Historical Theology: Continuity and Change in Christian Doctrine*. 1971. Reprint, Eugene, OR: Wipf & Stock, 2014.

———. *Jesus Through the Centuries: His Place in the History of Culture*. New Haven: Yale University Press, 1999.

———. *Luther the Expositor: Introduction to the Reformer's Exegetical Writings*. St. Louis: Concordia, 1959.

———. *The Melody of Theology: A Philosophical Dictionary*. 1988. Reprint, Eugene, OR: Wipf & Stock, 2014.

———. *The Mystery of Continuity: Time and History, Memory and Eternity in the Thought of Saint Augustine*. Charlottesville: University Press of Virginia, 1986.

———. *Obedient Rebels: Catholic Substance and Protestant Principle in Luther's Reformation*. New York: Harper & Row, 1964.

———. "The Past of Belief: Reflections of a Historian of Doctrine." In *Future of Belief Debate*, edited by Gregory Baum, 29–36. New York: Herder & Herder, 1967.

———. "Patron Saint for Christian Unity." *Liguorian* 54 (1966) 15–17.

———. "A Personal Memoir." In *Orthodoxy and Western Culture: A Collection of Essays Honoring Jaroslav Pelikan on his Eightieth Birthday*, edited by Valerie Hotchkiss and Patrick Henry, 29–44. Crestwood: St. Vladimir's Seminary Press, 2005.

———. "Preface." In *The Reality of Christianity: A Study of Adolf von Harnack as Historian and Theologian*, by G. Wayne Glick, xi–xiii. New York: Harper & Row, 1967.

———. *The Riddle of Roman Catholicism: Its History, Its Beliefs, Its Future*. Nashville: Abingdon, 1959.

———. *The Shape of Death: Life, Death and Immortality in the Early Fathers*. Nashville: Abingdon, 1961.

———. "Theology without God." In *Encyclopaedia Britannica Year Book*, 671. Chicago: Encyclopaedia Britannica, 1966.

———. "Tradition, Reformation, and Development." In *Frontline Theology*, edited by Dean Pearman, 101–7. Richmond: John Knox, 1967.

———. *The Vindication of Tradition: The Jefferson Lecture in the Humanities for 1983*. New Haven: Yale University Press, 1984.

———. *Whose Bible Is It? A History of the Scriptures through the Ages*. New York: Penguin, 2006.

———. "Wilhelm Pauck: A Tribute." In *Interpreters of Luther: Essays in Honor of Wilhelm Pauck*, edited by Jaroslav Pelikan, 1–8. Philadelphia: Fortress, 1968.

Peter, Carl. Review of *The Christian Tradition: A History of the Development of Doctrine*. Vol. 2, *The Spirit of Eastern Christendom (600–1700)*, by Jaroslav Pelikan. *Worship* 49 (1975) 313.

Preus, James. *From Shadow to Promise*. Cambridge: Harvard University Press, 1969.

Radano, John. *Celebrating a Century of Ecumenism: Exploring the Achievements of International Dialogue*. Grand Rapids: Eerdmans, 2012.

Bibliography

"Ralph W. Beeson, 'Samford's Greatest Donor', Dies at 89." http://media.sbhla.org.s3.amazonaws.com/7043,17-Oct-1990.PDF.

Rea, Robert. *Why Church History Matters: An Invitation to Love and Learn from Our Past.* Downers Grove: IVP Academic, 2014.

"Remembering Leading Reformation Scholar David C Steinmetz." https://www.ivpress.com/press-releases/2015/remembering-leading-reformation-scholar-david-c-steinmetz.

"Samford University Names Beeson School of Divinity." http://media.sbhla.org.s3.amazonaws.com/6708,08-Dec-1988.pdf.

Schaff, Philip. *Creeds of Christendom.* 3 vols. Grand Rapids: Baker, 1977.

Second Vatican Council. *Unitatis Redintegratio: Decree on Ecumenism.* Edited by Austin Flannery. Collegeville: Liturgical, 2014.

Serene, Eileen. Review of *The Christian Tradition: A History of the Development of Doctrine.* Vol. 3, *The Growth of Medieval Theology (600–1300)*, by Jaroslav Pelikan. *Religious Studies* 16 (1980) 489–90.

Smith, James, and George Huntston Williams. "'In Defense of Church History': A Minister with Historical Perspective." In *The Contentious Triangle: Church, State and University*, edited by Rodney L. Peterson and Calvin Augustine Pater, 399–411. Sixteenth Century Essays & Studies 51. Kirksville: Thomas Jefferson University Press, 1999.

Souther Baptist Convention. "The Baptist Faith and Message." http://www.sbc.net/bfm2000/bfm2000.asp.

Sproul, Robert. "The Manhattan Declaration: Why Didn't You Sign It, R.C.?" *Ligonier* (blog), August 12, 2009. https://www.ligonier.org/blog/the-manhattan-declaration/.

Steinmetz, David. "Abraham and the Reformation: The Controversy over Pauline Interpretation in the Early Sixteenth Century." In *Medieval and Renaissance Studies*, edited by G. M. Masters, 10:94–114. Chapel Hill: University of North Carolina Press, 1984.

———. "Aquinas for Protestants: What Luther Got Wrong." *The Christian Century* 122.17 (2005) 23–26.

———. "Asbury's Doctrine of the Ministry." *Duke Divinity School Review* 40 (1975) 10–17.

———. "The Baptism of John and the Baptism of Jesus in Huldrych Zwingli, Balthasar Hubmaier and Late Medieval Theology." In *Continuity and Discontinuity in Church History Festschrift for George H. Williams*, edited by F. F. Church and Timothy George, 169–81. Leiden: Brill, 1979.

———. *The Bible in the Sixteenth Century.* Durham, NC: Duke University Press, 1990.

———, ed. *The Bible in the Sixteenth Century.* Duke University Monographs in Medieval and Renaissance Studies 11. Durham: Duke University Press, 1996.

———. "Calvin among the Thomists." In *Biblical Hermeneutics in Historical Perspective*, edited by M. S. Burrows and P. Rorem, 198–214. Grand Rapids: Eerdmans, 1991.

———. "Calvin and Abraham: The Interpretation of Romans 4 in the Sixteenth Century." *Church History* 57 (1988) 443–55.

———. "Calvin and His Lutheran Critics." *Lutheran Quarterly* 4.2 (1990) 179–94.

———. "Calvin and Melanchthon on Romans 13:1–7." *Ex Auditu* 2 (1986) 74–81.

———. "Calvin and the Absolute Power of God." *Journal of Medieval and Renaissance Studies* 18.1 (1988) 65–79.

Bibliography

———. "Calvin and the Divided Self of Romans 7." In *Augustine, the Harvest, and Theology (1300–1650): Essays Dedicated to Heiko Augustinus Oberman in Honor of his Sixtieth Birthday*, edited by Kenneth Hagen, 300–312. Leiden: Brill, 1990.

———. "Calvin and the Irrepressible Spirit." *Ex Auditu* 12 (1996) 94–107.

———. "Calvin and the Monastic Ideal." In *Anticlericalism in Late Medieval and Early Modern Europe*, edited by Peter A. Dykema and Heiko A. Oberman, 605–16. Leiden: Brill, 1992.

———. "Calvin and the Natural Knowledge of God." In *Via Augustini: Augustine in the Later Middle Ages, Renaissance and Reformation: Essays in Honor of Damasus Trapp*, edited by Heiko A. Oberman and Frank A. James III, 142–56. Leiden: Brill, 1991.

———. "Calvin and the Patristic Exegesis of Paul." In *The Bible in the Sixteenth Century*, 100–118. Duke Monographs in Medieval and Renaissance Studies 11. Durham: Duke University Press, 1990.

———. "Calvin as an Interpreter of Genesis." In *Calvinus Sincerioris Religionis Vindex: Calvin as the Protector of the Purer Religion*, edited by Wilhelm H. Neuser and Brian G. Armstrong, 53–66. Sixteenth Century Essays & Studies 36. Kirksville: Sixteenth Century Journal Publishers, 1997.

———. *Calvin in Context*. New York: Oxford University Press, 2010.

———. "The Catholic Luther: A Critical Reappraisal." *Theology Today* 61.2 (2004) 187–201.

———. "Divided by a Common Past: The Reshaping of the Christian Exegetical Tradition in the Sixteenth Century." *Journal of Medieval and Early Modern Studies* 27.2 (1997) 245–64.

———. "Doing History as Theologians." *Catholic Theological Journal* 50 (2015) 174–80.

———. "For the Sake of the Gospel." Seminary Chapel sermon. Duke Divinity School, Durham, NC, May 17, 1997.

———. "Heiko Oberman and John Calvin." *The Calvin Theological Review* (2007) 347–52.

———. "The Intellectual Appeal of the Reformation." *Theology Today* 57.4 (2001) 459–72.

———. "John Calvin on Isaiah 6: A Problem in the History of Exegesis." *Interpretation* 36 (1982) 156–70.

———. "Luther and Calvin on Church and Tradition." *Michigan Germanic Studies* 10.1–2 (1984) 98–111.

———. "Luther and Formation in Faith." In *Educating People of Faith*, edited by John Van Engen, 253–69. Grand Rapids: Eerdmans, 2004.

———. "Luther and Staupitz: The Unresolved Problem of the Forerunner." In *Ad fontes Lutheri: Toward the Recovery of the Real Luther. Essays in Honor of Kenneth Hagen's Sixty-Fifth Birthday*, edited by Timothy Maschke et al., 270–280. Milwaukee: Marquette University Press, 2001.

———. "Luther and Tamar." *Lutheran Theological Seminary Bulletin* 73.1 (1993) 3–15.

———. "Luther and the Ascent of Jacob's Ladder." *Church History* 55 (1986) 179–92.

———. "Luther and the Late Medieval Augustinians: Another Look." *Concordia Theological Monthly* 44 (1973).

———. *Luther in Context*. Bloomington: Indiana University Press, 1986.

———. "The Making of a Theologian." *Lancaster Theological Seminary Bulletin* 4 (1969) 11–20.

———. "Mary Reconsidered." *Christianity Today*, December 5, 1975. https://www.christianitytoday.com/ct/1975/december-5/mary-reconsidered.html.

Bibliography

———. *Memory and Mission: Theological Reflections on the Christian Past.* Nashville: Abingdon, 1988.

———. *Misericordia Dei: The Theology of Johannes von Staupitz in Its Late Medieval Setting.* Studies in Medieval and Reformation Thought 4. Leiden: Brill, 1968.

———. "The Nature of Luther's Reform." *Duke Divinity School Review* 44 (1979) 3–13.

———. "The Nature of Ordination in the Light of Tradition." *Lancaster Theological Seminary Bulletin* 3 (1969) 8–19.

———. "The Necessity of the Past." *Theology Today* 33 (1976) 168–76.

———. "Ordination and the Theology of the Cross." *Duke Divinity School Review* 41 (1976) 36–40.

———, ed. *Oxford Encyclopedia of the Reformation.* 4 vols. New York: Oxford University Press, 1996.

———. "The Protestant Minister and the Teaching Office of the Church." *Theological Education* (1983) 45–59.

———. "The Re-Evaluation of the Patristic Exegetical Tradition in the Sixteenth Century." In *The Bible as Book: The First Printed Editions*, edited by Kimberly Van Kampen and Paul Saenger, 135–42. London: The British Library, 1999.

———. "Reformation and Conversion." *Theology Today* 35 (1978) 25–32.

———. "The Reformation and the Ten Commandments." *Interpretation* 43.3 (1989) 256–66.

———. "The Reformation in Context." Reformation Heritage Lecture given at Beeson Divinity School, Samford University, Birmingham, Alabama, October 31 to November 2, 1995.

———. *Reformers in the Wings: From Geiler von Kaysersberg to Theodore Beza.* Philadelphia: Fortress, 1971.

———. "Religious Ecstasy in Staupitz and the Young Luther." *Sixteenth Century Journal* 11 (1980) 23–37.

———. "The *SBJT* Forum." *The Southern Baptist Journal of Theology* 13.1 (2009) 110–12.

———. "The Scholastic Calvin." In *Protestant Scholasticism: Essays in Reassessment*, edited by Carl R. Trueman and R. Scott Clark, 16–30. Carlisle, UK: Paternoster, 1999.

———. "Scholasticism and Radical Reform: Nominalist Motifs in the Theology of Balthasar Hubmaier." *Mennonite Quarterly Review* 45 (1971) 123–44.

———. "Scripture and the Lord's Supper in Luther's Theology." *Interpretation* 37 (1983) 253–65.

———. "The Superiority of Pre-Critical Exegesis." *Ex Auditu* 1 (1985) 74–82.

———. "The Superiority of Pre-Critical Exegesis." In *A Guide to Contemporary Hermeneutics: Major Trends in Biblical Interpretation*, edited by Donald K. McKim, 65–77. Grand Rapids: Eerdmans, 1986.

———. "The Superiority of Pre-Critical Exegesis." *Theology Today* 37 (1980) 27–38.

———. *Taking the Long View: Christian Theology in Historical Perspective.* Oxford: Oxford University Press, 2011.

———. "Theological Reflections on the Reformation and the Status of Women." *Duke Divinity School Review* 41 (1976) 197–207.

———. "Theology and Exegesis: Ten Theses." In *A Guide to Contemporary Hermeneutics: Major Trends in Biblical Interpretation*, edited by Donald K. McKim, 27. Grand Rapids: Eerdmans, 1986.

Bibliography

———. "The Theology of Calvin and Calvinism." In *Reformation Europe: A Guide to Research*, edited by Steven E. Ozment, 211–32. St. Louis: Center for Reformation Research, 1982.

———. "Uncovering a Second Narrative: Detective Fiction and the Construction of Historical Method." In *The Art of Reading Scripture*, edited by Ellen F. Davis and Richard B. Hays, 54–65. Grand Rapids: Eerdmans, 2004.

———. "Wide-Angle Historian: Jaroslav Pelikan, 1923–2006." *The Christian Century* (2006) 31–33.

———. "Woe to Me if I Do Not Preach the Gospel!" *Duke Divinity School Review* 39 (1974) 1–9.

Steinmetz, David, and David Bagchi. *The Cambridge Companion to Reformation Theology*. Cambridge: Cambridge University Press, 2004.

"Summaries of Doctoral Dissertations." *The Harvard Theological Review* 72.3–4 (1979) 315–22.

Sweeney, Douglas. *Edwards the Exegete: Biblical Interpretation and Anglo-Protestant Culture on the Edge of the Enlightenment*. New York: Oxford University Press, 2017.

"The Theological Declaration of Barmen." *Church & Society* 85.6 (1995) 124.

Thomas, Terry. Review of *Luther in Context*, by David Steinmetz. *Currents in Theology and Mission* 15 (1988) 282.

"Timothy George." http://archives.sbts.edu/the-history-of-the-sbts/our-professors/timothy-george/.

"Timothy George." https://www.beesondivinity.com/directory/George-Timothy.

"Timothy George." https://www.crossway.org/authors/timothy-george/.

Treier, Daniel. "The Superiority of Pre-Critical Exegesis? Sic Et Non." *Trinity Journal* 24 (2003) 77–103.

Wax, Trevin. "Reformation Theology or Theologies? A Conversation with Timothy George (Part 2)." *The Gospel Coalition* (blog), October 17, 2013. https://www.thegospelcoalition.org/blogs/trevin-wax/reformation-theology-or-theologies-a-conversation-with-timothy-george-part-2/.

———. "Theology of the Reformers: A Conversation with Timothy George (Part 1)." *The Gospel Coalition* (blog), October 16, 2013. https://www.thegospelcoalition.org/blogs/trevin-wax/theology-of-the-reformers/.

Wilken, Robert. "Credo: Historical and Theological Guide to Creeds and Confessions of Faith in the Christian Tradition." *First Things* 143 (2004) 39.

———. "Jaroslav Pelikan and the Road to Orthodoxy." *Concordia Theological Quarterly* 74 (2010) 93–103.

———. "Jaroslav Pelikan, Doctor *Ecclesiae*." *First Things* 165 (2006) 19–21.

———. *Remembering the Christian Past*. Grand Rapids: Eerdmans, 1995.

Williams, George Huntston. "A Century of Church History at Harvard, 1857–1957." *Harvard Divinity School Bulletin* 23 (1957–58) 85–102.

———. "Christology and Church-State Relations in the Fourth Century." *Church History* 20 (1951) 3–33.

———. "Church History: From Historical Theology to the Theology of History." In *Protestant Thought in the Twentieth Century: Whence and Whither?*, edited by Arnold Nash, 147–80. New York: Macmillan, 1951.

———. "The Church, the Democratic State, and the Crisis in Religious Education." *Harvard Divinity School Bulletin* 14 (1949) 35–61.

———. "Current Trends in Unitarian Theology." *The Christian Register* 124 (1945) 41–44.

Bibliography

———. "The Elect of All Mankind." *The Christian Register* 134 (1955) 23, 26.

———. *The Harvard Divinity School: Its Place in Harvard University and in American Culture.* Boston: Beacon, 1954.

———. "'In Defense of Church History' A Minister with Historical Perspective." In *The Contentious Triangle: Church, State and University,* edited by Rodney L. Peterson and Calvin Augustine Pater, 399–411. Sixteenth Century Essays & Studies 51. Kirksville: Thomas Jefferson University Press, 1999.

———. "An Intellectual Portrait of Pope John Paul II." *Worldview* (1979) 21.

———. "Introduction." In *Spiritual and Anabaptist Writers: Documents Illustrative of the Radical Reformation,* edited by George Huntston Williams, 1:19–38. The Library of Christian Classics 25. Philadelphia: Westminster John Knox, 1957.

———. "Issues Between Catholics and Protestants at Mid-Century." *Religion in Life* 23 (1954) 163–205.

———. Message to National Youth Pro-life Coalition Convention, November 23, 1973, Box 10, Folder 18, George Huntston Williams Papers, Andover-Harvard Theological Library, Harvard Divinity School, Harvard University, Cambridge, MA.

———. *The Mind of John Paul II: Origins of His Thought and Action.* New York: The Seabury, 1981.

———. "The Ministry in the Ante-Nicene Church." In *The Ministry in Historical Perspective,* edited by H. Richard Niebuhr and Daniel D. Williams, 27–59. New York: Harper, 1956.

———. *The Norman Anonymous of 1100 A.D.: Toward the Identification and Evaluation of the So-Called Anonymous of York.* Harvard Theological Studies 18. Cambridge: Harvard University Press, 1951.

———. "Priest, Prophet, and Proletariat: A Study of the Theology of [Sin in] Paul Tillich." *Journal of Liberal Religion* 1 (1940) 25–37.

———. *The Radical Reformation.* Philadelphia: Westminster, 1962. Reprint, Kirksville: Truman State University Press, 1995.

———. "Religious Education in a Pluralistic Democracy." *Religious Education* 50 (1955) 38–44.

———. "Religious Residues and Presuppositions in the American Debate on Abortion." *Theological Studies* 31 (1970) 10–75.

———. "Reluctance to Inform." *Theology Today* 14 (1957) 229–55.

———. *Rethinking the Unitarian Relationship with Protestantism: An Examination of the Thought of Henry Hedge.* Boston: Beacon, 1949.

———. "The Sacramental Presuppositions of Anselm's *Cur Deus Homo.*" *Church History* 26 (1957) 254–74.

———. "The Sacred Condominium." In *The Morality of Abortion,* edited by J. T. Noonan Jr., 1–60. Cambridge: Harvard University Press, 1970.

———. "The Spontaneous Missionary Church: A Lesson from Ancient Church History." *Laity* 4 (1957) 3–14.

———. "Studies in the Radical Reformation (1517–1618): A Bibliographical Survey." *Church History* 27 (1958) 124–60.

———. "What Has Jerusalem to do with Athens?" *Universalist Leader* (1953) 195–97.

"Williams, George Huntston (1914–2000)." https://www.harvardsquarelibrary.org/biographies/george-huntston-williams/.

Williams, Rowan. *Why Study the Past? The Quest for the Historical Church.* Grand Rapids: Eerdmans, 2005.

Bibliography

Wills, Gregory. *Southern Baptist Seminary 1859–2009*. New York: Oxford University Press, 2009.

Wojtyła, Karol. "Ut Unum Sint." *Origins* 25 (1995) 51–72.

Woodbridge, John. "Timothy George and Evangelical and Catholics Together: An Evangelical Perspective." In *Worship, Tradition, and Engagement: Essays in Honor of Timothy George*, edited by David Dockery et al., 262–77. Eugene, OR: Pickwick, 2018.

Vanhoozer, Kevin. "Scripture and Tradition." In *The Cambridge Companion to Postmodern Theology*, 149–69. New York: Cambridge University Press, 2003.

———. "Sola Scriptura, Tradition and Catholicity in the Pattern of Theological Authority," In *Worship, Tradition, and Engagement: Essays in Honor of Timothy George*, edited by David Dockery et al., 109–28. Eugene, OR: Pickwick, 2018.

Vincent of Lérins. "*Commonitorium*, no. 22." In *A Select Library of the Nicene and Post-Nicene Fathers of the Christian Church*, edited by Philip Schaff and Henry Wace, 11:131–56. 14 vols. Grand Rapids: Eerdmans, 1969–76.

von Ranke, Leopold. *The Theory and Practice of History*. Edited by George G. Iggers and Konrad von Moltke. Translated by Wilma A. Iggers and Konrad von Moltke. New York: Routledge, 2010.

Yarnell, Malcom. "Calvinism: Cause for Rejoicing, Cause for Concern." In *Calvinism: A Southern Baptist Dialogue*, edited by Ray Clendenen and Brad Waggoner, 73–95. Nashville: B&H Publishing, 2008.

———. *The Formation of Christian Doctrine*. Nashville: B&H Publishing, 2007.

www.ingramcontent.com/pod-product-compliance
Lightning Source LLC
Chambersburg PA
CBHW050817160426
43192CB00010B/1800